what KIDS NEED *to* SUCCEED

FOUR FOUNDATIONS OF ADULT ACHIEVEMENT

by Andrea Patten *and* Harry S. Patten

Williamstown, Massachusetts

International Standard Book Number: 0-9761923-0-6
Library of Congress Catalog Control Number: 2004097796

Note: This publication contains the ideas and opinions of its authors. It is
sold with the understanding that neither the authors nor the publisher are
engaged in rendering professional services in the book. Readers requiring
personal assistance or advice should contact a qualified professional. The
authors and the publisher specifically disclaim any liability, loss, or risk,
personal or otherwise, which is incurred as a consequence, either directly
or indirectly, of the use and application of the contents of this book.

The publisher offers discounts on this book when ordered in quantity for
bulk purchases, special sales and certain fundraising.

Please contact us at: specialsales@whatkidsneedtosucceed.com

To Hannah, with love.

Thanks

The authors are grateful to our family, friends and colleagues. You helped take this project from an idea to a book by generously sharing stories, time, comments, ideas and support to help us think and write more clearly. Mark, 'mega thanks' for the time, the training, support and vision. Jan for transcribing hours of interviews — and for the title! Brian and John for proving our point and Hannah for making it really matter.

TABLE OF CONTENTS

PART FOUR —
FOUNDATION #3 DEVELOP DISCIPLINE

PART FIVE —
FOUNDATION #4 GIVING BACK

FOREWORD

My life and my work have taken me on many wonderful and amazing adventures. I am gratified and humbled at the number of dreams I have lived out, the goals I have attained, and the rich, fulfilling friendships that are mine.

But one adventure stands out for me. It has brought me immeasurable joy and has inspired me to grow in ways that I didn't know were possible. And, since you're reading this book, it's probably an adventure that you and I share.

I'm talking about being a parent. The twenty four-hour-a-day, seven-day-a-week job that is among the most wonderful experiences anyone can have. It is also a staggering responsibility.

Not just the responsibility of the daily routines and the soccer practices and the college funds and the school plays... but the responsibility that comes when you realize that everything your child knows about the world, from what it means when the leaves fall in autumn to how to treat other people, will start with you. Your attitudes and the lessons you pass on will be the most crucial factors for what this new, small human being makes of his or her life.

As many of you know, I am a big fan of setting goals. I encourage everyone to set big, audacious goals — and lots of them. At least 101. Passion-fired goals for every area of your life... involving everything and everyone you care about.

How does one do that? It starts with a picture. Start at the end. Picture the results you want — in vivid, graphic, multisensory detail — before starting to write down your goals. That's what I've been teaching for years.

So you can imagine the excitement I felt when I first sat with Harry and Andrea Patten to talk about their book. I was thrilled. Not simply because I thought it would be a wonderful work (which it is), but also because that's what this book does. It starts with the end in mind. Harry and Andrea have done the heavy lifting for you... reading, researching and interviewing successful adults from a variety of different disciplines and discovering the childhood experiences that bind them together.

What Kids Need to Succeed *is about raising successful adults. And that's what parenting is about, in the end: raising successful adults. Raising happy, financially secure, fully realized human beings who treat themselves and others with respect and compassion, who act with integrity, work hard, who pursue their passions and find joy in life — and pass the same qualities on to their own children.*

As parents, that's all we aspire to. But I can tell you from personal experience, you can't do it merely by diving headfirst into the daily childrearing routine and reacting as challenges come along. You need a plan. What Kids Need to Succeed *gives you one.*

I believe this book reflects the wishes of many people who were lucky enough to be raised by terrific parents: we want to share what we were taught, because those lessons have brought such joy to our own lives. We want to pass on the knowledge that our parents passed down to us — and we don't want to limit it to just our own kids.

Harry and Andrea have distilled the critical lessons of childhood down to Four Foundations: Work Hard, Refuse to Fail, Have Limits, and Give Back. They form an underlying structure upon which many other valuable lessons and skills can be built. I think every parent has a duty to share these essential values with his or her child.

What a marvelous insight, that the most important character builders in a child's life become the cornerstones of a successful adult life! And by success, I don't just mean financial success (and neither do Harry and Andrea). The lessons of What Kids Need to Succeed *give young people the framework to pursue literally* anything *as adults, from financial prosperity to activism, art to engineering. The key is that with the Four Foundations ingrained since they were old enough to walk, whatever they do, they'll do it with persistence, hard work, discipline, integrity, compassion, and love. That's success in anyone's book.*

And let's not forget: they'll hopefully pass the same wisdom on to their own children. These lessons are generational, wonderful gifts that parents give to their children again and again. I am privileged to have met many of the people in this book and have seen the lessons work in their lives. Harry's father gave him the gift, Harry gave it to Andrea, and Andrea sent it on to her son. And now they give the same gift to you in the hopes that you'll be inspired by the stories, anecdotes, and plain good advice between these covers. Inspired to create a plan for your children built around teaching the Four Foundations. Inspired to give your children the gifts that virtually every successful adult I have ever spoken with also received as a child.

In the end, that's really what it means to be a parent. It's doing the best you can to give your child the tools to be the best human being possible. Whether that means being a captain of industry or a kindergarten teacher isn't up to you. Whether they have the character to make their choices with courage, passion, and determination is. Harry and Andrea have given you a splendid toolbox. Open it and build something extraordinary.

Mark Victor Hansen, Co-creator
Chicken Soup for the Soul and
The One Minute Millionaire
Newport Beach, California

CHAPTER 1

What's the Difference between Ordinary and Extraordinary?

N o, darling," said the petite, impeccably dressed woman seated at the front of the room. "My mother didn't raise me alone because my father died — he was hospitalized after he tried to kill my older brother and sister."

The answer was delivered matter-of-factly, and with such warmth and compassion that if the student who asked the question was uncomfortable, she managed to conceal it from the crowd of more than five hundred as the next student posed another tough question to a member of the panel.

Brigadier General Sherian Grace Cadoria had been to the State Department on any number of occasions during her distinguished career as the army's first black female nontraditional line general. And although these audience members, in their own way, were as powerful as the military and government leaders who were her colleagues and peers, everything about this visit was different.

A Mother's Strength

Audience members sat spellbound with tears in their eyes as Shereé spoke about the events that had brought her to the podium that day to celebrate her induction into the Horatio Alger Association of Distinguished Americans.

Her journey — in which hardship came long before victory — began on January 26, 1943, in Marksville, Louisiana, where her parents worked as tenant farmers. When she was only three months old, her father was kicked in the head by a mule, resulting in serious injury. Although the family did the best they could to care for him at home, the severity of his condition led to bizarre and dangerous behavior.

One night, unable to ignore the misfirings in his brain, Shereé's father tied rocks around the necks of two eldest children and tried to drown them. Fortunately, he was stopped, and Shereé's mother, Bernice, with the kind of courage and practical strength that characterized her life, committed her husband to a hospital where he would remain until his death.

If Shereé's life story were submitted as a possible TV movie, executives would probably reject it as overly dramatic or unbelievable. But truth is often far more compelling than fiction, and her family faced more than its share of obstacles.

An Early Learner

The next obstacle came quickly: Bernice and her three children were evicted by the farmer who owned their tiny home. After all, without a male head of household, the family would certainly be unable to meet its obligations to the landowner at harvest time.

But Bernice knew otherwise. She packed up her family's few possessions and moved to a nearby town, where she found a farm owner willing to take a chance on them. And as soon as Sheré could walk, she was given her own sack to fill — really just a pillowcase — and joined her family in the cotton fields. Now, everyone knows that a three-year-old can't possibly pick cotton... everyone but Sheré and her family. This would be the first in a long series of "impossible jobs" at which the little girl would excel, despite being told, "No, you can't."

In the segregated South, the most fortunate black children were well schooled in the unparalleled value of education. With little else under their control, their parents made certain they understood that no one could ever take away what was in their heads. So, lacking child care, Bernice sent little Sherian to school with her older siblings while she worked to feed them. The nuns made a place for the young girl to play quietly in the back of the room while the older kids studied their lessons. But Sheré absorbed all that was going on around her, and when she was finally old enough to be enrolled in school, she began in the third grade — another pattern she would repeat many times.

Into the Military

The years passed, and Sheré entered college. She had always idolized her older brother, a navy man, and hoped that she would find a way to follow in his footsteps. In her junior year at Southern University in Baton Rouge, she was selected by the Women's Army Corps to represent the university at the College Junior Program. The experience gave her a glimpse of what was ahead if she aspired to a military career.

"It was tough. It was awful. But it was also fascinating," she says. She spent four weeks at Fort McClellan in the summer of

1960 and entered the army in 1961, with a direct commission as a first lieutenant in the Women's Army Corps.

Despite the fact that society did not look kindly upon black women who chose to step into new roles, the driven young woman and the army were a perfect match. The military discipline was reminiscent of Bernice's early teachings. However, Shereé soon found that even her impeccable performance in the army could not shield her from the turmoil of the time: the terrifying Ku Klux Klan demonstrations outside the base, or the insult of being refused service at a nearby hamburger stand.

Nevertheless, looking back, Shereé says, "Most of the prejudice I encountered had more to do with being a woman in a man's world than with being black."

A Galaxy of Honors

Eventually, Sherian Grace Cadoria became the first female African-American general in the history of the U.S. Army. When she retired in 1990 after twenty nine years of service, she left behind an amazing legacy and a career full of firsts: the first woman to command an all-male battalion in Vietnam, the first to lead a criminal investigation brigade, the first black woman director of the Joint Chiefs of Staff, and the first woman admitted to elite army schools, the Command and General Staff College and the U.S. Army War College.

I was in the audience the day that General Cadoria became a member of the Horatio Alger Association. My dad was one of the community leaders moved to tears as he listened to her story. And as we listened, we both recognized that the hard lessons of her childhood had made her many adult achievements possible. We'd seen them before in other high achievers.

Growing up black, female, fatherless, and in dire poverty, young Sherian Cadoria was told that she was less than others. But her mother, her older siblings, and the nuns who facilitated her education made her believe that she was strong, smart, capable, and that she absolutely *owed* the world the gift of her many talents. Their teachings, encouragement, and challenges enabled the young girl to grow into someone who was able to thrive at the highest level.

Such backgrounds are common to all the Horatio Alger honorees and others who achieve at the highest levels. These people weren't blessed with special gifts from birth. They weren't prodigies. They weren't simply luckier than anyone else. The difference between them and others is that from earliest childhood, they had to strive to overcome, and to work harder and smarter than anyone else. And their parents, either unwilling or unable to shield them from adversity and failure, helped them to *learn and to grow from these experiences.*

It all started in their early years. That is what made them different, and as adults, made them extraordinary success stories. That recognition — that parents shape their children's futures by passing on "Four Foundations" in early childhood — was the genesis of everything you're about to read. And Brigadier General Sherian Grace Cadoria is testimony to that truth.

CHAPTER 2

Learn from the
People You Want
Your Kids to Be Like

Most books about raising kids focus on kids — universal needs, developmental milestones, and the like. But I can't think of another one that starts with the generals, the CEOs, the mega-best-selling authors and the All-Stars and looks *back* at the childhood lessons that gave them their edge. In this book, you'll eavesdrop on candid conversations among high-achieving adults, and incorporate some of their insights and lessons into the wisdom that you share with your own kids.

In the pages to come, you'll get to know people who have overcome difficulties in their lives and gone on to achieve excellence. You'll get an inside look at the lives of people who bring high standards and value everywhere they go. These people are a joy to spend time with. They're trustworthy, hardworking, and inspire achievement in others. Some of them are old enough to reflect back on the value of early life experiences. Others are still quite young.

You'll read stories of people who take on ordinary tasks in an extraordinary manner. You'll also start to recognize the superstars in your own life and discover the things their parents taught them that other parents neglected. As you do, you'll start to see the same critical traits in them.

What are the common traits and childhood experiences shared by top achievers? How did they acquire the skill or drive that has taken them to the top as adults? Many of those answers lie in these pages.

But first, it's important to know who's telling the story....

CHAPTER 3

Andrea *Who?*

Writing a book was one of my most vivid childhood dreams. As far back as I can remember, I cut and folded paper, stapling a different-colored cover onto the carefully numbered pages of my latest story. Sometimes they were even illustrated. I can still remember the feeling I got when I printed "by Andrea Patten" underneath the title of my latest imaginary best-seller.

Until now a great deal of my working life has been spent with families in trouble, working under the broad umbrella of human services. I'm a decent researcher, a good problem solver, and you probably won't find anyone who gets more pleasure out of taking an idea, a budget, and a set of goals and making them into a tangible reality.

But the most important, best job I've ever had is being a mom. Today my son is a wonderful man — smart, hardworking, moral, and well mannered — and that ties directly to the telling of this story.

Lessons from My Father

Most of my work has involved innovation: adapting DWI program materials for nonreaders, adding a wives' support group to a Vietnam vets' program, spearheading a substance abuse assessment program in a child protection organization, and more.

I was sort of a "human services entrepreneur," a quality I know came from the lessons and values my father instilled in me. These experiences also led me to some tough questions. Why do certain people succeed as adults? Why do others fail? What separates those who are motivated by adversity from those who become helpless in its wake? I began to see that the answers I sought were in stories.

"If you find it in your heart to care for somebody else, you will have succeeded."

— Maya Angelou

I learned the power of being a storyteller as I spoke to prospective donors and members of the community. I discovered the profound effect a human story could have on its audience.

At the same time, in an entirely different setting, my father was asking the same questions, conducting his own interviews, and coming to some compelling conclusions.

Dad and I share an insatiable curiosity about people and their stories. We began to see patterns in the lives of people who became happy, productive, and successful, and of those people who seemed powerless to control life's events. After a while, we realized that we were hearing the same stories and that it made sense to work together to share them.

I realize now that it's all the same great story... and that for more than forty years I've been doing research on it. It's time to tell it.

CHAPTER 4

The Four Foundations

The American dream begins with the American family.

— Sen. Barbara A. Mikulski (D, Maryland)

My father has always been fascinated by successful people. I remember him telling me how as a young boy he was drawn to the stories of Abe Lincoln and Ted Williams, imagining himself in their shoes. Character, innovation, and hard work leading to great success — the American Dream stories.

Dad also loves good books. He would tell us about his mother reading him great stories like *The Adventures of Tom Sawyer* and *Black Beauty*, how he could almost see Black Beauty straining under the heavy load, and, sixty years later, remembers the thrill he felt when Beauty found a new home.

But I can't tell you exactly how he decided to write this book. Whatever it was, three important interests — success, kids, and books — converged to become a single, galvanizing thought: *The lessons parents teach their children in early childhood make the difference between high achievement and mediocrity in their adult lives.*

He examined this thought from several angles: his own upbringing, his hiring record, and his successes and failures as a parent. Dad's vision turned into a passion to share this information with other parents — especially young parents who are worried about the ways their input affects the future success or failure of those they love the most. Together, we decided to write a book to pass on the secret that's shaped multiple generations of our family.

The Secret of Adult Success

The secret is so simple and powerful that it might escape you at first. It's this: All highly successful adults share a common childhood foundation: four crucial values taught to them by their parents. For your child to reach his or her full adult potential, throughout childhood he or she must

1. **Refuse to Fail** — Those who get knocked are expected to get back up and try again. That's the behavior that gets rewarded and reinforced — not the whining.
2. **Work Hard** — If they want something, they have to earn it.
3. **Develop Discipline** — There are clear, high expectations for behavior. They are known and followed. There is no room for negotiation.
4. **Give Back** — They show their appreciation for help and kindness, treat others with compassion and respect, and make giving to others a priority.

There may be people who lead perfectly satisfying lives without these "Four Foundations." But I can state with confidence that children who do not learn these lessons will find it almost impossible to achieve their peak potential. And that doesn't need to happen.

CHAPTER 5

There's No
Time to Waste

God gave us two ends — one to sit on and one to think with. Success depends on which one you use; heads, you win — tails, you lose.

— Anonymous

Many parents of young children are tired and overwhelmed. There are meals to fix, bills to pay, and laundry to do. It's tempting to tune out well-meaning relatives and friends when they tell you how quickly the early years with your children will fly by. But they're right.

Time is short, and there is much to do in order to equip your kids with a strong base for a fulfilling adult life. No matter how busy you are, one fact remains: If you want your children to learn the lessons they'll need to be successful adults, you must teach them the Four Foundations daily. The sooner you start, the better.

Many of the people Dad and I will introduce to you have triumphed in the business world. However, the skills and attitudes they possess have value far beyond the workplace. Discipline, the ability to persevere in the face of hardship, a well-developed work ethic, and generosity can benefit any physical fitness program, charitable work, and academic or artistic endeavor with which your child becomes involved.

As this book has taken shape, Dad and I have had the opportunity to discuss our observations with people in a variety of fields. We've found that all successful people share a common background. Early in life, there was discipline, a strong work ethic, a helping hand, and a challenge to overcome.

CHAPTER 6

Harry S. Patten's
Magic Moment

Something happened to twelve-year-old Harry S. Patten at the All-American Hometown Memorial Day Parade in his hometown of North Conway, New Hampshire. He saw many wonderful things on that sunny May morning, but he also had a life-altering experience. He was captivated by the sight and sound of the visiting marching band's brass section. "I knew then and there that I not only had to play the trumpet, but I had to march down Main Street in one of those fantastic-looking uniforms," he says. It didn't take him long to convince his parents that he should abandon piano lessons in favor of the trumpet.

There was just one small problem with Harry's plan: the town had no marching band. But to the budding entrepreneur, this was no big deal. He did something that he continues to do to this day: he created something. He approached his closest buddies, who agreed they should start their own band. "We had very little musical training, but the vision of marching together down Main Street motivated and inspired us," he says. So Junior

Nilsen and Dave Newcomb took up the clarinet, Bruce Snair the drums, and Billy Nash the trombone. After lots of loud but enthusiastic practices, the official North Conway Community Center Band was born.

Now there was the other part of the boys' vision: uniforms. After all, how could a *real* band march through town in dungarees and T-shirts? In order to attain their goal, the band members needed sharp, new John Phillip Sousa–style uniforms with gold braid on the shoulders. At two hundred dollars per uniform, it looked like that part of the dream might remain unfulfilled.

Not if Harry had anything to say about it. At his urging, he and the other boys began telling their story to local merchants. Impressed by the boys' drive and passion, the gas station owner gave fifty dollars, the owner of the appliance store gave fifty dollars, and so on. Before long, they had raised the money they needed. Harry's father, who worked for a clothing company, got a special deal and personally sized every child for a made-to-measure uniform.

Soon, North Conway residents were treated to the sight and sound of their very own homegrown marching band, complete with professional attire. "I don't know who was more proud, the band members, the parents, or the town business owners," Harry says. "To this day, I still get goose bumps when I watch *The Music Man.*"

The Advantage of Growing Up Poor

But there's more to the band story than civic pride. It illustrates Harry's character and exemplifies the guiding principles of his life and the core idea of this book: given the gifts of discipline, a strong work ethic, the ability to rise to challenges, and a desire to contribute, a child can accomplish anything. "I was the catalyst in getting the marching band started," Dad says, "because I had been taught that I could do anything I wanted if I was willing to work hard."

If you could press a button and fast-forward through my dad's life, you would see that little has changed. He started a real estate company that became Patten Corporation, the country's largest buyer and seller of rural and recreational land. In 1985, he took the company public, and the $100 million-a-year enterprise was applauded by *The Wall Street Journal, Forbes, Fortune,* and many other publications. In 1995, he retired...temporarily. In less than a decade, the company he started "in retirement" has eclipsed Patten Corporation.

Dad's is a real rags-to-riches story. He has always believed that the riches would never have been possible without the rags, or, what he calls "the competitive advantage of growing up poor."

Wait a second. Competitive advantage? Isn't childhood poverty nothing but hardship? Certainly many of today's American children, who want for nothing materially, would find parts of my father's upbringing unbearable. Dad was born in 1936 to my grandmother, Suzanne, and my grandfather, also named Harry. They married relatively late in life and chose to settle in a small town in northern New Hampshire.

North Conway was a magical place for a young boy to grow up: a classic small New England town, with white church steeples and clapboard houses, an old-fashioned Main Street, and a peaceful village green at its heart. Nestled in the Mount Washington Valley, the Swiss and Austrian immigrants who were helping found the American ski industry gave the town an international feel. But despite the idyllic setting, life wasn't easy. My grandfather (who was known as Grampa Pat) made a tough living selling made-to-measure clothing door-to-door for the Arthur B.

Nash Company. And when my dad was only about three, Grampa Pat fell from a stepladder and severely injured his back.

Breakfast Lessons

With Grampa Pat unable to work and Suzanne, a nurse, taking care of him full-time, the family's financial picture grew dim. One day, as my grandmother counted out change to pay Mr. Wentworth, the meat man, Harry spotted her handing him a penny. A bent penny.

"That was my special penny from my piggy bank! I embarrassed her, letting her know long and loud about her terrible mistake," he says. "I didn't realize until much later that she needed it just to pay the bill. It was the same for almost everybody in town at that time."

Harry remembers the exact day he realized his family was poor. "One Christmas morning, I flew down the stairs, delighted to find that Santa had brought me several new trucks," he says. "But later that morning, as I was playing with my trucks, I turned them over and realized to my disappointment that they were my old trucks, carefully repainted so I would have something under the tree." It took him years to realize that his mother had been motivated by love.

But Harry's most cherished childhood memories are of his many breakfasts with Pat. As a door-to-door salesman, my grandfather worked evenings, so in the mornings he cooked breakfast for his son, and they talked. About everything. "Breakfast lasted an hour, sometimes two," Harry says. "It was the most important time of the day for us. I learned about my dad's values — love, responsibility, vision, goal setting, and dreams. He talked to me about being successful."

The Great Chicken Massacre of 1943

Great role models have the power to change lives, and Harry was fortunate to have his father as his own first mentor. Grampa Pat believed in instilling self-reliance and a strong work ethic in his boy from early childhood because he knew firsthand that Harry would need them to survive and flourish in a sometimes-harsh world.

One of the earliest lessons was in entrepreneurship. When Harry was seven, my grandfather bought him a dozen chickens and the equipment to care for them. "He told me they were my responsibility and that they would die if I did not feed and water them every day," Harry says. "When they started to lay, I collected the eggs, sorted them into small, medium, and large, and sold and delivered them." But the new business was not without strings attached; Harry had to repay his father for the startup costs. "After I made a weekly payment to the 'Harry Owes Dad Fund,' I could keep whatever money remained," he says.

Unfortunately, just as the debt was paid off and it looked like Harry was ready to rake in the cash, a neighbor's dog killed most of the chickens. "I was crushed and financially ruined," he says today with a grin. "But like many other childhood lessons, that experience prepared me to face challenges later in life."

The lessons continued, always focused on discipline, overcoming obstacles, and the need to work hard to make good things happen. When Harry wanted a baseball glove, his father showed him how he could sell house nameplates door-to-door to earn the money. He sent for the sales kit, sold the nameplates for $2.98 each, got $1 for each sale, and got his glove. "I also got the sales skills that have been the foundation for my business success," Harry says.

The Difference between Success and the Rest

Growing up in a family with little money meant that my father had to work for absolutely everything he wanted. He learned early that there are no free rides.

Harry's successes are a direct result of the lessons and values that his father instilled in him as child: hard work, overcoming adversity, discipline, and giving back to others. But over the years he's noticed a disturbing trend: many of today's parents are not passing on those same values to their own children.

Concerned that the priceless lessons of his childhood were being ignored by later generations, Dad started asking, "What makes the difference between successful and unsuccessful adults?" He began to seek answers by reviewing his own hiring experiences, later moving on to wider research and interviews with successful people from many fields.

Dad made sure to pass on these same important life lessons. Those lessons — and the research, interviews, and endless questions they inspired — are at the heart of this book. For any parent who wants to raise a child with the strength and values to achieve real adult success, the precepts are absolutely essential. "Parents who have a genuine interest in preparing their children to become successful adults are in a race against time," he says.

CHAPTER 7

What Is Success?

Or, Is a Good Day for

Donald Trump a Bad

Day for Mother Teresa?

suc·ceed (sək-**sēd**) *v.*

1. To come next in time or succession; follow after another; replace another in an office or a position.

2. To accomplish something desired or intended.

I'm surprised by some of the questions I'm asked when I talk about this book. The one I get the most often is, "What do you mean by *success?*"

Despite their protestations to the contrary, there are plenty of people who define success as one thing: having a lot of money. That is certainly one definition of success, but it's not what we're talking about here.

You may be surprised to find that neither Dad nor I define success as having a certain job or a specific amount of money in the bank — unless that's one of your goals. We don't necessarily define success as being happy — unless, of course, that's one of your goals. In fact, Dad and I don't always define success the same way.

But when we talk about successful people, both of us include individuals who take responsibility for themselves, their lives, and their happiness. Rather than waiting for favorable circumstances, they make good things happen for themselves.

Though you'll encounter many definitions of success in this book, I wouldn't presume to define success for you or your child. That's *your* job.

What Is Success?

People have had their own definitions of success for centuries. This quotation has been attributed to Ralph Waldo Emerson and Bessie A. Stanley:

"To laugh often and much, to win the respect of intelligent people and the affection of children, to earn the appreciation of honest critics and endure the betrayal of false friends, to appreciate beauty, to find the best in others, to leave the world a bit better, whether by a healthy child, a garden patch, or a redeemed social condition; to know even one life has breathed easier because you have lived. This is to have succeeded!"

I interviewed Barbara Nolan, a stay-at-home mom who transformed herself into the VP of marketing for a public corporation. She shared her sense of satisfaction about having raised successful adults. "They're happy and independent. What else could I ask for?" she said. "I've done my job as a mother — they enjoy their live's and they are not dependent on anyone but themselves."

In addition to coauthoring the wildly successful *Chicken Soup for the Soul* series, Mark Victor Hansen is a well-known motivational speaker. He defines success as "creating a state of mind that allows you to achieve whatever it is you want."

Success Changes as Life Changes

When he was younger, much of Dad's definition of success was based on "not being poor." However, as his earnings reached a level that moved our family far beyond the survival level, there was room for that definition to change. He saw that financial success without health, friends, family, or giving back to the community was not what he wanted.

Today, he says, "Success is feeling happy and satisfied about life while progressing from one worthwhile goal to the next."

What's a better life or a worthwhile goal? That's up to you and your child. It could be earning a certain amount of money or buying a home. It could be achieving and maintaining a level of physical fitness, mastering a new sport, or participating in a race.

Maybe it's being accepted by a certain college, solving a research problem, or earning an advanced degree. It could be returning to school after a long absence, or developing a rich and rewarding spiritual life, or reading all the classics. Maybe it's having the passion to pursue an artistic vision, or creating positive change in the community.

As parents, it's our job to give our children the tools to go out and pursue whatever is meaningful to them. As long as they have the Four Foundations to rely on, they'll be able to make their way with confidence and pride, to define success for themselves.

Teach Kids to Celebrate Themselves

Talking about success makes some people insecure. We're trained to be modest, to downplay our passions and ambitions. Instead, parents should encourage children to take pride in their achievements, to take joy in what they care about, even in the hard, sweaty work that comes with any success story. Success is nothing to be ashamed of.

Succeed also means "to follow." All parents are preparing the next generation to take their place in the adult world. The ability to achieve their goals, pursue their passions, and stand on their own two feet is the greatest gift any parent can give a child.

I hope this book will help you examine your definitions of success — for yourself and for your children. In fact, before you go to the next chapter, take a minute and jot down your current definition of success. As time passes, note how that definition changes...but the Four Foundations your kids need to reach those goals don't.

PART ONE

THE FOUR DEADLY SINS OF PARENTING

CHAPTER 8

Childhood Success Doesn't Equal Adult Success

It is not giving children more *that spoils them; it is giving them more to avoid confrontation.*

— John Gray

My father had been chipping away at this book for years, with me often serving as devil's advocate. Over the years, our exchanges became a sort of thrust-and-parry as I searched for the flaws in Dad's idea:

"There are people who don't reach their highest potential who are relatively happy," I said once. "They'd be happier if they achieved all that they are capable of," he responded.

And so it went until one day I pointed out the glut of parenting books on the market. "There are hundreds of books out there about raising successful kids," I said.

Dad didn't hesitate. "Have you found any about raising successful adults?"

That was an "a-ha" moment for me. That idea, that there's a difference between raising good kids and raising good adults, ultimately brought us together to write this book.

Great Goal-Setters Start at the End

I had read plenty of parenting books, magazines, and articles. Some of the information was invaluable. I read page after page about how to manage potty training, promote attachment and administer time-outs. They tell you what to expect when you're

> *"My formula for success is rise early, work late, and strike oil."*
>
> — J. Paul Getty

expecting, when your kid's a toddler, and at every stage along the way. They teach you how to raise successful kids — *but no book talked about how to raise successful adults.*

Great goal-setters start at the end. They visualize what they want their lives to be like at a specific point in the future, and work backwards to the present, identifying the steps they need to take to make those goals reality.

But I don't remember reading a single piece on parenting that encouraged me to visualize the kind of adult I would like to raise, and determine the steps I had to take to ensure that my child would learn the skills needed to become that kind of adult.

Kids Masquerading as Adults

Think about the last frustrating interaction you had with another adult. You were expecting an adult interaction and were instead treated to something more akin to actions of an ill-behaved child — a missed deadline, a flimsy excuse, or self-centered behavior.

We have become a society of brats. We want what we want when we want it. When we make mistakes, we whine and point fingers instead of taking responsibility. When children don't get what they want, they throw tantrums. "Adults" file lawsuits.

Pick a problem: obesity, drugs, alcohol, skyrocketing personal debt, domestic violence, divorce. They are all fueled by the fact that many Americans want something for nothing, deny the consequences of their actions, refuse to be accountable, and are amazingly self-absorbed.

Making Things Easier Doesn't Do Kids Any Favors

But if you talk to the adults who are successful (or on their way to being so), you find that they were raised by parents who set goals and had a plan for reaching them. They are today's stars and tomorrow's superstars. Whether or not they know it, their parents gave them an incredible gift: the Four Foundations.

Keeping your eyes on the prize makes day-to-day parenting decisions much easier. A friend of mine had a child who, although extremely bright, was not a good student. After a series of frustrating and guilt-provoking parent-teacher conferences, this single mother, in the spirit of the Four Foundations, changed the rules.

Mother, teacher, and student attended the next conference. As instructed, the boy greeted the teacher, sat silently, and listened. The mother invited the teacher to talk to her as if the child were not there. The teacher gave her a list of things she could do to improve her son's grades. The mother said, "These aren't my grades. I've already completed the third grade. If my child misbehaves in your classroom, I want to know about it immediately. I promise you it will stop."

She continued. "When my son achieves success, he is going to know that it is through his own efforts, not yours or mine. I'm always available to help, but if he doesn't do the work, he should get a failing grade. I will not be in here asking you to change it."

Does that sound harsh? It's not. My friend was willing to sit down with her son every evening to review assignments, quiz spelling words, and check math — but only if he initiated it. She was not willing to sacrifice her child's future by letting him shirk his responsibilities. That would have been parenting to raise a successful child...not a successful adult.

Parenting with an Eye on the Future

My friend was able to be that kind of parent because she took the long view of parenting: that it was her job to raise a person who would have the skills to be successful all his life, not just to be a star in the third grade. With an eye to your child's future as your guiding principle, it's simple to apply the Four Foundations.

Parenting in this manner is simple but not easy. It's much harder than just giving in and making our kids happy in the short run. We feel better about ourselves. But isn't making the tough choices part of being a grown-up?

9

Don Dion,

Entrepreneur at an

Early Age

If you want to see what children can do, you must stop giving them things.

— Norman Douglas

Don Dion grew up in Maine, where it snows a lot in the winter. To earn spending money, he started lining up winter snow-shoveling jobs as soon as the autumn leaves began to turn. He got leads, quoted prices, and convinced people to use his snow-shoveling services. But after doing all the legwork to line up the jobs, Don hired people to actually shovel the snow.

"I'd go along and help them, but my biggest contribution was getting the jobs," he says. "I would charge by the driveway or walk, and split it, half-and-half, with the person who actually shoveled. I felt this was only fair since I had gotten the jobs in the fall. Without my earlier efforts, no one would have been earning anything."

A Fitting Role Model

With that kind of work ethic and ability to create opportunity, is it any wonder that Don was a multimillionaire, a successful lawyer, and CNN commentator by the age of forty? He gives a great deal of credit for those qualities to the example set by both his father and his grandfather.

"My grandfather had a little furniture store in Canada, and things weren't very good," Don says. "He had heard that things were better in America, but to get on the train and go there, you needed a trunk. So he saved, bought a big black trunk with a padlock, and filled it with rocks and newspapers, which he pretended were his wares for entry into America."

"What the vast majority of American children needs is to stop being pampered, stop being indulged, stop being chauffeured, stop being catered to. In the final analysis, it is not what you do for your children but what you have taught them to do for themselves that will make them successful human beings."

— Ann Landers

After Don's grandfather came to America, he worked in the mills during the day, and at night he and his friends dug house foundations by hand. Eventually, he bought a little furniture store, and Don's father went into business with him.

"Here's the thing," Don says. "When the store was supposed to open at eight, there was no chance of its opening at five minutes past. There were these rules that were never broken — no wavering and no excuses. From the day I was born, I was always around people who worked hard."

Don has lived the lessons of this book. Working hard to get what he wanted as a child didn't hurt him. Instead it taught him invaluable lessons and helped him develop determination, innovation, team building, and persistence.

Teach Determination

All the successful people we interviewed for this book worked and had responsibilities both inside and outside their homes. For their parents, part of "giving their children everything" was giving them the chance to work and learn the important lessons that work provides. When you interview the successful people in your own life, listen for the recurring themes and lessons. You'll find them similar from person to person.

Don started working when he was about ten. "I used to dust the furniture and wash the windows in my grandfather's store," he says. "I remember you had to put ammonia in the water because it was so cold in the winter. Raw ammonia, so the water didn't freeze. I'd do that two days a week. I always liked the fact that I was part of the business. As soon as I was in eighth grade, I started delivering the furniture and did that all the way through high school."

As parents, it's our duty to provide children with the tools to face and overcome life's obstacles. Developing a child's work ethic is a perfect way to begin. A great way to start is by giving your child jobs and making it clear that to get something means using brains, muscle, and determination. Don Dion is proof of that.

CHAPTER 10

Equality, Deadly

Parenting Sin #1

There are two great injustices that can befall a child.
One is to punish him for something he didn't do. The
other is to let him get away with doing something he
knows is wrong.

— Robert Gardner

Once upon a time, America was full of mean parents. They made their kids do household chores and eat dinner before dessert. They insisted that they chew with their mouths closed, take off their hats when inside, and call adults strange names like Mr., Mrs., Sir, or Ma'am. Nothing happened unless there was a *please* beforehand, and nothing else happened until a *thank you* was uttered.

These parents were strange in other ways, too. They went to work every day and lived within a written monthly budget. All the children completed assigned household chores to earn their allowance money.

When their kids grew up, they knew how to set up and maintain a household before they were thirty years old, how to start at the bottom and work their way up, and that it was important to give a good day's work for a fair day's pay. In other words, they were prepared to function as adults.

But some of those kids grew up and decided they didn't like the way they had been raised. Instead of being grateful for having the skills they needed to function, they resented being made to work. And when they had children, they were unwilling to "be the bad guy." So they changed the definition of good parenting to look like this:

- Children should never struggle or experience discomfort.
- Children are little adults entitled to equality with their parents and input into how the family is run.
- Kids should always be happy.
- We are our children's friends.

Parenting Is Not a Democracy

When we treat our children as equals, when we worry about being their friends instead of their parents, we fail them. Running little self-esteem farms, where the most important thing is that little Johnny feels good about himself, serves no one.

I'm going to crawl out on a limb and say that self-esteem may be overrated. It is not a cure-all. Haven't you met people without basic skills who seem to feel far too content with the status quo? The truth is, when children grow into adults who are able to care for themselves and others, they'll feel good about themselves. It

"Part of being a champ is acting like a champ. You have to learn how to win and not run away when you lose. Everyone has bad stretches and real successes. Either way, you have to be careful not to lose your confidence or get too confident."

— Nancy Kerrigan

won't be because someone else told them they should. That's true self-esteem.

Parents who fret over self-esteem worry that they'll stifle Junior's personality if they hold him to tough standards. They believe they'll damage their children if they use discipline, hard work, and giving as teaching tools. Such parents can become paralyzed and end up running little democracies where the children have as much say in how they're raised as their parents. Or worse, they end up with "pediarchies," little banana republics where the kids are really in charge.

A Few Truths

- Kids already have friends. They need parents.
- Children need strong adult leadership.
- Children and parents are not equals.
- Being upset or angry is not fatal.

Clear expectations and adult leadership grant children the opportunity to learn skills appropriate to their ages and to move gradually through the stages of healthy development.

Children are learning how to live. As a parent, you are more than their example. You're also their teacher, mentor, and coach. And just as a football coach sometimes needs to make the team run laps to enforce discipline or make players stronger, you need to show the same kind of firm leadership with your children. They may not like it, but they'll thank you for it later.

When they're grown, you'll have plenty of time to be friends.

CHAPTER 11

Overindulgence,
Deadly Parenting
Sin #2

Overindulgence is one of the most insidious forms of child abuse known to man.

— Dr. Phil McGraw

The lack of discipline and accountability in the upbringing of so many kids today is really part of a hidden epidemic of child abuse. It's "hidden" because it's often disguised as kindness. If you want to find out about this kind of abuse, put down the paper, turn off the TV, and go somewhere. Anywhere you can find parents and children in public.

Go to a Little League game, and you may see a star athlete throw a bat in frustration over a "bad call." A visit to a kindergarten class might reveal a teacher dreading recess, because simply dressing everyone to go outdoors has become a nightmare.

And you probably don't even have to think very hard to conjure up an image of the last tantrum you witnessed in the supermarket checkout line.

What Does It Mean to Give Your Kids Everything?

A big part of the problem is that the meaning of "giving your kids everything you didn't have" has changed in the last few decades. Parents have always wanted their children to have a better way of life than they did; that's natural. But in my father's age, and even

"Striving for success without hard work is like trying to harvest where you haven't planted."

— David Bly

in mine, that was not just about giving children more material things. Many households were supported by a single paycheck. The standard of living wasn't as high; much of what parents gave to their kids was love, attention, lessons, values, and morals. They still wanted their children to have a higher standard of living, but they also had the time to pass on important life lessons.

In many of today's families, both parents work outside the home. They have less time to spend with their kids. So now, instead of giving their kids time, guidance, and discipline, they give them computers, clothes, and cars. Instead of having to work for the things they want, many kids simply have to ask. Parents too tired from work or too guilty over the lack of time let kids get away with a lot of bad behaviors that lead to the development of bad habits. In some communities, there is competition to see which parents on the block can give their kids the most expensive stuff.

Kids are being overindulged to a dangerous extreme. When we give them everything they ask for (and many things they don't) in a misguided attempt to show them love, we handicap them emotionally and developmentally. They never learn the importance of work and sacrifice, and assume that things will always be handed to them and that someone will always come along to clean up any mess.

Some Kids Are Learning

But if you go back to the ballgame, the school, and the supermarket, you'll also find children who are learning to work, can accept discipline, and refuse to give up when things don't go their way.

At the ball field, you'll notice a marginal athlete who is allowed to play the required league minimum and not a single minute more. She's picking up the equipment, asking the coach how she can improve, and arranging extra practice for herself. If no one will work with her, she'll stay anyway, long after the game is over, practicing her swing.

Or you'll meet the kindergartener who is always the first one out to play, because she knows how to put on her own boots, hat, and coat. Or at the grocery store, you'll exchange hellos with the young grocery bagger who buys his own clothes and is saving every extra cent he earns to pay his own college tuition. You know, the one who does the job quickly, looks you in the eye, and doesn't squash your bread?

Human beings feel best when challenged to do more and rise to the occasion. That's how we're built. A reward earned through hard work is always sweeter than one just given. The highest achievers are those who, as children, earned what they got and learned to see setbacks as challenges.

Washerwoman-turned-philanthropist Oseola McCarty saved $280,000 over the course of her lifetime by washing and ironing other people's clothes. She lived frugally and saved scrupulously, and ended up donating $150,000 of her savings to the University of Southern Mississippi. "There's a lot of talk about self-esteem these days," she says. "It seems pretty basic to me. If you want to feel proud of yourself, you've got to do things you can feel proud of. Feelings follow actions."

Holding Some Things Back

So there's hope. We can start redefining what it means to give our kids "everything." It's more important for a child to spend time with his father every Saturday, learning to take care of household chores, than it is for him to have a new computer. Wise parents understand that, even if they can afford to lavish their children with material possessions, they need to *hold things back deliberately* and provide their kids with the motivation and opportunity to work for what they want. Those are the parents raising successful adults.

CHAPTER 12

No Consequences,

Deadly Parenting

Sin #3

Today we're going to learn a little Parental Math. Ready? In a healthy family, the equations look like this:

If A = Didn't complete my expected household chores
Then B = Don't get my allowance

If A = Didn't do the homework and got a failing grade
Then B = Meet with the teacher and work harder to pass

If A = Didn't work hard enough to make the team
Then B = Watch from the sidelines and wait until next year

But in a family where parents don't allow their children to experience the consequences of their actions, the equations look like this:

If *A* = Didn't complete my expected household chores
Then *B* = Get my allowance anyway

If *A* = Didn't do the homework and got a failing grade
Then *B* = Mom meets with my counselor to blame my teacher

If *A* = Didn't work hard enough and didn't make the team
Then *B* = Dad accuses the coach of bias and threatens to sue the league

What's Your Reaction?

For every action, there's an equal and opposite reaction. That's a law of physics, and it's a law of sound parenting. In the first family, where there are clear expectations and codes of conduct, you can bet the children know that if they mess up, they're going to face the music. Nobody's going to bail them out.

In the second family, the parents don't hold their children accountable. Often, the parents take their children's failure to make the team or get the best grade as a reflection on themselves. So they make excuses, step in on their child's behalf, and often make things worse. They also create adults who are unwilling, and maybe even unable, to take responsibility for their actions. That's the result of parents who commit the sin of No Consequences.

"You may have to fight a battle more than once to win it."

— Margaret Thatcher

In a misguided effort to enhance children's self-esteem, many adults accept unacceptable behavior from children. Instead of meeting bad behavior with consistent discipline, many adults are choosing the path of least resistance and letting kids "get away with it." As a result, we're teaching them how to fail.

When we don't allow children to struggle and overcome adversity, we fail to teach them that actions have consequences. When we don't make them accountable for their behavior, we fail to teach them that good manners are mandatory. When we make excuses for them, we fail to teach them that they are responsible for the things they are able to do themselves.

Mastering the Math

Have you ever run into an adult who seems to think the laws others live by don't apply to her? Someone who shows total disregard for others and when she screws up, immediately points the finger at everyone but herself. Surely, someone else must be responsible! There's a 99% chance that she was raised by parents who refused to let her experience any negative consequences.

None of us wants to raise a child who grows up to be that kind of adult. But mastering the math of parental physics means first understanding that the Four Foundations are like muscles: to build them, you must work them. If you buy your child a weightlifting set but do all the lifting for him, he won't develop any muscles. And if you try to teach your child about work ethic, overcoming adversity, discipline, and giving back, but don't let him learn from his failures, you're shortchanging him.

The equation of a smart, caring, strong parent looks something like this:

A = Clear boundaries, expectations, and rules of conduct established early on.

B = Consistent consequences for breaking the rules or failing to live up to expectations.

C = Firm and fair enforcement of rules and consequences.

D = Appropriate assistance or guidance.

E = Unconditional love.

y = A child who works harder to fulfill expectations.

$$(A + B + C / D) \times E = y$$

Cruel to Be Kind?

It's hard to watch kids fail. Every instinct screams at us to help them, to step in and do things for them. But by doing so, you end up denying them one of the greatest thrills a young person can know: figuring out what went wrong and working to succeed next time, *all on their own.*

CHAPTER 13

Inaction,

Deadly Parenting

Sin #4

Parents who are unaware of the importance of the Four Foundations don't realize that to raise a high-achieving, fulfilled adult, they must have a plan. Sometimes what we don't do can hurt a child more than what we do.

Those who commit the sin of inaction parent by the seat of their pants, ignoring their own most valuable life lessons. They seem to think that self-sufficient, hardworking, determined children "just happen" without any special preparation.

As a result, they don't take a long view of parenting. Unless they make a conscious decision to impart the Four Foundations of work ethic, overcoming adversity, discipline, and giving, they're likely to raise their children like steering rudderless ships: weaving from one compass point to another. One month they're strict; the next they're not holding their kids accountable for anything.

A Master's Degree in Life

Think of this as creating a master's degree curriculum in living for your children. It's educating them as they grow, according to a blueprint, presenting new challenges as they develop and mature. Smart parents sit down and make a conscious plan for the upbringing of their children, one that includes the Four Foundations.

Think of it like writing a business plan, only this is the most important business of all: the education and development of high-quality human beings who can thrive on their own.

Questions you might ask as part of this "business plan" include:

- What values do we want to pass on to our kids?
- What lessons from our own childhoods must be shared or avoided?
- What kind of people do we want our children to be?
- What are the three most important qualities we want our children to possess?

Good parenting takes planning, awareness and action. My father's insight — that the highest achievers share common childhood experiences — shows parents the way to give their children the ability to thrive as adults.

CHAPTER 14

Redemption
and the
Four Foundations

C an a caring parent avoid the deadly parenting sins? We think so. There is a light at the end of the tunnel — four lights, to be exact.

It doesn't matter if you think you're part of the problem. It doesn't matter if, up to now, you've never given a second thought to how to teach your children the values that will make them successful adults. All that matters is that now you know how to proceed. And if you start while your kids are young, you can give them the tools to achieve whatever they want to in their lives.

The key is to begin today to teach your children the values represented by the Four Foundations:

1. Persistence and the ability to overcome adversity
2. A strong work ethic
3. Solid, consistent discipline
4. Giving back to others

The Four Foundations are a cure for the epidemic. Children imprinted with these qualities at a young age can grow up to be self-starting, ethical, hardworking adults with a great deal of integrity, strong values, and tremendous self-confidence. The Four Foundations form a solid base on which you and your child can stack a whole variety of values, lessons, and life experiences.

CHAPTER 15

The Imprinting

Advantage

The beginning is the most important part of the work.

— Plato

"Imprinting" is a term that was first coined in the 1930s, by Konrad Lorenz, to explain a bonding phenomenon that takes place between young animals and their caregivers during an early, critical period. While the theory has been further developed over time, we use it here to refer to the impact of early experiences on a child's subsequent growth and development.

Horse trainers offer good examples of imprinting. Within minutes of a foal's birth, humans pick up its feet and tap the bottoms, simulating future handling by the blacksmith. Electric clippers are run near the ears. Fingers in the mouth simulate the bit that will be worn in the future. In the hours just after birth, the foal is handled a lot.

After those few hours, the foal and its mother usually go out to live in a pasture, often for as much as a year. When yearlings that were handled as foals begin their training, they are not afraid of clippers or the blacksmith. They easily accept a bit and are ready to learn.

Those without that early exposure come in from the pasture wary of humans and are difficult to teach.

Humans Imprint Life Lessons

The same thing happens to human animals. We "imprint" character traits and habits upon our children through experience and example. A child who is imprinted with love learns to be a loving adult. A child who is continually shown that, with hard work and persistence, he can accomplish anything becomes a self-motivated, confident adult.

If you approach parenting from this perspective, it becomes clear that everything you do has an effect on your child's imprint and the development of his or her character traits. So it's clear that it's crucial not only to teach, but also to lead by example and show — not just tell — children the benefits of hard work, discipline, and determination.

CHAPTER 16

The Magic Years

When Everything's

Possible

Lost time is never found again.

— Proverb

What if someone walked into the room right now and told you that you had three years to become fluent in Chinese? Would you panic? At a minimum, I'll bet you would feel some doubt about your ability to reach the goal. At best, you'd recognize three years of backbreaking work ahead of you.

Yet every year, millions of three-year-olds accomplish the same task almost effortlessly. In fact, with proper exposure, a small child living anywhere can learn several languages, achieve fluency, and speak without an accent in a way that older children and adults simply cannot, no matter how hard they work.

The Early Years Are the Learning Years

This doesn't apply only to language. The fact is, human beings learn more easily in early childhood than at any time in their lives. In a widely quoted study of language acquisition, noted MIT linguist Noam Chomsky reported that in the period from age 2 to 15, the average child will increase his or her vocabulary at the rate of one new word *every 90 minutes*. Children are built to soak up new knowledge and skills.

The bottom line is, kids must learn the Four Foundations during the period we call "the magic years." The older we become, the more difficult it is to acquire a skill for which there is no foundation. And when it comes to basic values and personality traits, those who don't "get it" during the magic years, rarely catch up. Children need the opportunity to learn *now*.

Like Riding a Bicycle...

The common expression, "It's like riding a bicycle," refers to a complicated skill or set of skills mastered early on and retained,

"If you raise your children to feel that they can accomplish any goal or task they decide upon, you will have succeeded as a parent and you will have given your children the greatest of all blessings."

— Brian Tracy

more or less intact, throughout life. The implication of the phrase is that if someone learned to ride a bike as a child, no matter how long it has been, he or she can still hop on and ride. It's something we don't question.

That concept remains true in almost every area of life. Whether it's earning money, playing a sport, or facing the consequences of one's actions, the skills mastered during the prime learning years remain easy and natural.

But those who must learn these skills as adults will never have the same fluency as those who learned while growing up. Think about accident victims who must relearn activities such as standing, walking, or talking. What is effortless for a child can be a Herculean ordeal for an adult.

Early Lessons Remain Easy and Natural

Nature gives all animals a window of opportunity in which to learn everything they need to become fully functional adults. For some, the time is very brief. In a few short months, baby birds learn to fly and feed themselves. Lion cubs take several years to learn to hunt, kill, and survive on their own in the wild. Thankfully, humans get a bit longer than that.

Adult skills and passions can often be traced back to early experiences, interests, and play. Lots of people can relate to trying to master golf or tennis as adults. Dad says he can go to any golf course or tennis club, observe the players, and always know who played the sport as a child. Try it yourself. Ask the high handicapped golfers whether they learned to golf as a child. I'll bet you already know the answer. My brother is a better golfer than Dad, and our kids are even better. Guess who started earlier?

Is Your Child's Window Still Open?

Childhood is a fleeting yet crucial opportunity to help young people develop strengths that will support them in their adult years. Parents are the chief architects and builders of childhood opportunity. Pathways developed in this period support all the learning that will follow. All childhood messages, positive and negative, become part of us, either aiding or hindering us.

If you don't impart critical lessons to your son or daughter in childhood, your child will never completely make up for it as an adult. Time is short, and there is so much to learn. Don't miss a teachable moment!

CHAPTER 17

Some Candid

Thoughts

Do not free the camel of the burden of his hump; you may be freeing him from being a camel.

— Gilbert K. Chesterton

- It's normal to second-guess yourself. Find a mentor, preferably someone who has raised a child who has become the kind of adult you want your child to be. Share your doubts with the mentor — not with your kids, and not with parents who let their kids run roughshod over them.
- It's your job to set the standards and limits. It's your child's job to test them. And he'll do anything, from tears and tantrums to accusations like, "You don't love me!" to get what he wants.
- Sometimes (okay, often) when you do the right thing, your children won't like it. They might tell you that they hate you, cry, or pout. Get used to it. Parenting is not a popularity contest.

- When your child cries, you will feel pain. You'll both get over it. If you want her to learn to put things in perspective, you've got to show her how to do it. It's not your child's job to make you feel better.

There is no job more important than preparing your kids to become adults. Give yourself a break. Keep that long view in mind, apply the Four Foundations, and you'll always know you're giving them the best possible start.

PART TWO

FOUNDATION #1

REFUSE TO FAIL

CHAPTER 18

The Adversity

Advantage

As loving parents, our natural instinct is to shield children from adversity. We go out of our way to protect them. We steer them away from competition as a way to avoid the pain of losing. We send them to schools with noncompetitive grading systems to bolster their self-esteem.

These practices ignore a basic human truth: adversity is a wonderful teacher. Now a noted author, speaker, and teacher, Dr. Wayne Dyer spent his early years in foster homes. Dave Thomas, founder of Wendy's, grew up in an orphanage. They had to learn to accomplish things for themselves when they were young, and those difficulties helped to build character and the drive to succeed.

If You Love Them, Let Them Struggle

Childhood adversity can take many forms: conflict with friends, failure to make the team, bombing an important test, living with poverty or illness, or the loss of a family member through death or divorce. It might be a speech impediment, poor eyesight, or a learning disability. It doesn't matter. Successful people rise above adversity.

We cannot live our children's lives for them, but we can provide the tools they need to survive and progress. When life throws your child a curve, it's important to allow him to search for a solution.

Easier said than done. It's hard for any parent to resist the urge to "make it better," even if letting a child get back up after a fall means making a stronger adult. Let children struggle through tough times using their mental, emotional, and physical abilities. Doing so isn't being neglectful. It takes courage and discipline. Allowing your children to struggle for themselves is being a foresighted, caring parent.

Obstacles Strengthen

Overcoming little obstacles makes us stronger and readies us for bigger challenges. Your belief that your child can do so is demonstrated not by words, but by supporting his efforts with minimal interference. How many times have you heard a young child cry, "I can do it myself!" Let them. Mastering new skills enhances self-confidence. Overprotection retards coping skills. We cannot — and should not — shield children from all of life's hard knocks, but we can show them how to deal with hardship.

Helping children learn to overcome adversity is a supremely loving act. Protect them from serious harm, but don't shield them from these necessary experiences, even though they may hurt. I hope that your children will never face terrible hardships or tragedies, but that you can instead use life's inevitable bumps and disappointments as opportunities for growth.

When your child gets hurt and cries as if the world is ending, it takes tremendous self-discipline to breathe deeply, assess the situation, and respond calmly. If you play down the injury, your child will almost always relax, lose the fear, and be back out playing in minutes. There's an art to offering only the help that is needed without turning simple situations into high drama.

There is an interesting paradox in this kind of parenting. What might appear on the surface to be abandoning a child to her own devices really relieves her of the burden of adult concerns. When a parent is grown up enough to do the hard things, like letting a child struggle, he grants that child the freedom to be a child.

The child who auditions for a play and is not chosen might discover that he is not cut out for drama, and will turn to some other pursuit that's a better match for his time and abilities. Or the love of theater might run so deep that he becomes motivated to find a different niche, such as writing or set design. But without experiencing the initial defeat, how would he find that out? Failure often shows us truths about ourselves... truths that most of us would not willingly seek out, because they're usually at least a little unpleasant.

Losses Teach

Kids' defeats also provide wonderful opportunities for us to remind them that we love them unconditionally, that trying new things is a great adventure, and that it's important to face defeat with grace. Adversity also presents a chance to introduce children to what may be one of life's most important questions: Why did I fail, and how can I do better the next time?

Learning to face struggles builds a foundation for effective problem-solving abilities in adulthood. Years from now children probably won't remember who won the lead in *Our Town*, but they will remember that a trusted adult had the confidence that they would survive the experience and reap its lessons.

High achievers have the ability to fall, get up, and still win the race. Losers use life's roadblocks as excuses to quit. The difference between success and failure is often as simple as how we view the inevitable obstacles along the way. Are they barriers? Or stepping-stones? Or, as John Wooden, legendary UCLA basketball coach, was known to say, "The team that makes the most mistakes wins."

Although the number varies from source to source, it is reported that Thomas Edison was once asked if he felt discouraged by his 1,073 failures en route to inventing the electric lightbulb. His response: "I did not fail. I found 1,073 ways not to do it."

Dr. Ben Carson, the nation's leading pediatric neurosurgeon, was born into poverty, yet reached the pinnacle of his profession. A devoted father, he feels that is it important for parents who have achieved success to create situations that allow their children to challenge adversity and learn its lessons.

When speaker and Internet marketing guru Tom Antion talks about his father, his love, respect, and gratitude are clear. An immigrant with only three years of formal education, Sam Antion gently introduced his son to the concepts of challenge and overcoming adversity. How? By cleverly placing pillows and other objects between the newly mobile child and his toys!

Help children discover their own solutions and the well of strength and resourcefulness inside them. As a parent, you will be rewarded with the satisfaction of watching your child develop confidence, self-esteem, and a determined, can-do attitude.

CHAPTER 19

Butterfly's

First Job

Adversity is the state in which man most easily becomes acquainted with himself, being especially free of admirers then.

— Samuel Johnson

Nature offers many examples of the value of struggle. A caterpillar hibernates in a chrysalis. Upon discovering this odd-looking residence, one might be tempted to "help" it become a butterfly by cutting into the structure and creating a ready exit.

Naturally, the 'butterfly prospect' will take the easiest way out, crawling through the new opening. But will it ever be able to unfurl its wings and fly? Will it ever become a butterfly? Struggling to get free of the chrysalis builds the strength the insect needs. What looks like a painful process is a vital step on the road to becoming a butterfly.

I'm sure that, if asked, the 'butterfly prospect' would tell us it doesn't want to work its way out of the chrysalis. That it's scary. And too hard.

So Mother Nature doesn't ask for input. Caterpillars simply undergo this process. It doesn't matter how anyone feels about it. It just *is*. If you look around the rest of the animal kingdom, you'll find similar examples of built-in struggle: chicks breaking out of their eggs, helpless baby sea turtles making a tortuous crawl toward the surf, salmon struggling upstream to spawn.

It's Survival

Nature doesn't put these barriers in the way of her creatures to be cruel. Animals that pass the test survive to pass their genes on to the next generation, improving the species. Nature favors those who struggle.

The fact is, once children become adults, their first test is survival. The adult world doesn't say, "Well, you tried hard, so even though you got lazy and botched your new job, we'll keep you on." Instead, it's "You're fired." It's Darwinian — those who can produce and make things better get to stay. By not being shielded from adversity, children learn what it takes to survive, and to thrive.

One of the greatest lessons we can teach our children is to live their lives with the ability to face fear and go beyond, to persevere and accomplish goals.

CHAPTER 20

Graduating from the School of Hard Knocks

A gem cannot be polished without friction, nor a man perfected without trials.

— Chinese Proverb

L et's continue my father's story.... When Harry was growing up, if he wanted something, he had to work for it. He held a variety of jobs, including door-to-door sales, yard maintenance, and working as a carpenter's helper. "I'm sure I groused about working as much as any kid would," he says. "At the time I didn't realize that I was getting a tremendous head start!"

He graduated with honors from Kennett High School in Conway, and went on to major in psychology at the University of New Hampshire. While still in college, he got married and became a dad, so he adjusted his school schedule to accommodate a full-time job — selling Kirby vacuum cleaners door to door.

"My Greatest Opportunity"

"In my senior year, the company's vice president offered me a chance to become the Kirby distributor for the Providence, Rhode Island area. With a second child on the way, my choice was clear," said Harry.

Things went well until a recession rendered many of his customers unable to pay their notes. He was forced into bankruptcy. "I was devastated," he says. "I now had three kids to support, and not much time to find a way to do so. We moved to Virginia so I could take a job as a sales manager for a land development company. As I have found with so many successful people, my greatest failure provided the seeds of my greatest opportunity."

He returned to New England to manage the company's new Northeast Division, where he learned enough about the business to start a company of his own. He started American Land and Development Company with wonderful results.

The company continued to expand, was renamed Patten Corporation, and in 1985 was listed on the New York Stock Exchange. Sales reached more than $100 million per year, and Harry served as company president and chairman of the board until his retirement in 1995.

The Golden Weeks

As I said earlier, my father's "retirement" lasted a few weeks. He's started multiple new companies that have surpassed his old one. Why? Because hard work and the satisfaction that come from achieving are a part of who he is. He's better at it and enjoys it far more than any of his wide variety of recreational interests.

From childhood, Harry learned that the only way you fail is to give up, and that if you want anything in life, you'd better be prepared to make it happen. I'll let him conclude:

"I am very fortunate. Hard work and a good example from my parents gave me the foundations needed to move from poverty to wealth," he says. "I've met fascinating people — salespeople, athletes, businesspeople — from all walks of life. And invariably, I've found that when someone impresses me with the way they do

Legendary UCLA basketball Coach John Wooden defined success as "peace of mind which is a direct result of self-satisfaction in knowing you did your best to become the best you are capable of becoming."

their job, we share a common history. I know right away that they faced obstacles during their childhood...and that they overcame them. They are disciplined, determined, hardworking, and they share their good fortune with others."

Dad's final point: "Growing up poor in America, before social welfare programs, proved to be a great privilege. It taught me many priceless lessons."

CHAPTER 21

Paul and Jim

All men dream, but not equally. Those who dream by night in the dusty recesses of their minds wake in the day to find that it was vanity. But the dreamers of the day are dangerous men, for they may act their dream with open eyes, to make it possible.

— T. E. Lawrence

To illustrate the importance of learning to outwit and out-work obstacles, Dad tells a story about two young men, Paul and Jim. They held the same position in his company, but ended up with very different results.

"Paul graduated near the top of his class with an MBA from a prestigious northeastern university. He was impressive in his interview — handsome, impeccably dressed, and well mannered. He seemed have all the right ingredients to become a sales star.

"His job performance was another story. He was often late for work, struggled to meet quotas, and had trouble working with

67

others. Even though Paul appeared to have the 'right stuff,' he lacked the discipline and the drive to succeed. Sadly, I had to fire him.

"At about the same time, Jim came looking for a job and some advice on how to improve his life. I almost dismissed him because of his tattered clothes and dirty fingernails. Remember that saying about appearances being deceiving?"

Driven to Have a Different Future

"But I noticed the intensity in Jim's eyes when he spoke about his eagerness for the job. Jim had grown up in a small coal-mining town in West Virginia. His grandfather had worked in the mines and died of black lung disease at forty two. His dad followed the same path and at fifty, could barely walk or breathe. By the time Jim was thirteen, a third generation had started 'in the hole.' He was determined he would not pour his life and health into a mine shaft as his father and grandfather had done.

"So I took a chance and hired Jim. Within six months, he became the top salesman in the company, earning more money in that period than he had in his entire working life.

"People of mediocre ability sometimes achieve outstanding success because they don't know when to quit."

— George E. Allen

"After many years of hiring 'Pauls and Jims,' I began to analyze the differences between people who fail and those who succeed. I read biographies and conducted interviews with successful people. They confirmed my belief that lessons learned as children set the stage for adult achievement.

"Jim hadn't had any of the so-called advantages of Paul — the education, the expensive clothes, the 'look.' What he did have was a childhood marked by tough lessons. Struggle lit a fire in his belly, and that was his ultimate advantage."

Daily Goals, a Lifetime of Results

Dad told me that each week, Grampa Pat set goals for himself. Every Monday after breakfast, he paid his bills and went to the bank to make a deposit. Then he left to start the workweek without a penny in his pocket. If he didn't make a sale on Monday morning, he couldn't even buy lunch. Talk about confidence and motivation.

Can-do people like Grampa Pat and Dad are driven to reach their goals. They are self-motivated, confident, and they believe that failure is not an option. They have the ability to overcome obstacles and get back on the right path. They appear to be lucky, but they cause and create their own rewards.

The most lasting gifts of childhood are found in the struggles and lessons that make us strong. Whether we prepare our kids for adulthood or we protect them into failure, our example is the most powerful teacher they will ever have.

CHAPTER 22

She Couldn't

Hear Anyone Say

"You Can't"

My life is my message.

— Gandhi

Motivational speaker Elienne Lawson knows seven languages and plays the piano. Take a look at her bright smile, her drive, and her fashion-model good looks, and you would never know that to get where she is today, she's climbed over a whole lifetime's worth of roadblocks.

The daughter of a minister and a business executive, Elienne was raised to believe that she could do anything she wanted to do as long as she was willing to pay the price. That approach helped her develop both a strong work ethic and discipline. When she made bad choices, there were consequences from which she was not shielded. When she worked hard, there were rewards.

Early on, she developed a strong preference for the rewards. In second grade, she learned of an opportunity to be a student ambassador to Russia. Her parents told her she could go...*if* she earned the money for it. So she produced a direct mail piece that enabled her to collect about one dollar each from six hundred people, and earned her trip.

Waking Up Blind and Deaf

When she was about nine, her family moved to the eastern US. Not long after that move, Elienne contracted viral meningitis and fell into a coma. Doctors told her parents that she would most likely die. "When I woke up, I was angry," she says now. "I had heard what they were saying; they shouldn't have hurt my parents that way!"

Elienne woke up — but she woke up blind and deaf. "My vision eventually came back, but my hearing was totally shot," she says. "I was treated with a lot of steroids, and I gained sixty pounds. So here I was, starting out in a new school, deaf *and* fat. Kids can be cruel." Elienne was teased unmercifully. Out of all the challenges she's faced, it's only the memory of her classmates' cruelty that still threatens to bring tears.

Too Smart to Be Deaf?

But she still had her powerful intellect, and she put it to good use. "Since even the geeky kids wouldn't be friends with me, I had lots of time to study," she says. She excelled at her studies. The result? Underperforming classmates' parents called the school and accused her of cheating. They said she couldn't really be deaf. On a few occasions, she even had to retake exams. She was furious. "I wanted the parents and some teachers to take those exams, too — so I could beat them!" she says.

"All my growth and development led me to believe that if you really do the right thing, and if you play by the rules, and if you've got good enough, solid judgment and common sense, that you're going to be able to do whatever you want to do with your life."

— Barbara Jordan

Elienne found herself facing another challenge: to attend the college of her choice, she needed a foreign language. But her school informed her that deaf people couldn't learn foreign languages. She eventually convinced them to allow her to continue studying Latin (which she had studied since the fifth grade), because most of the course was written rather than spoken.

But Elienne had a burning desire to learn French. "I wasn't allowed in the class, but I eventually found a teacher in college who was willing to work with me one-on-one," she says, beaming. "My French is much better than the kids who had to learn in a big group."

Her Greatest Asset

Let's add things up. When Elienne went into her coma, she spoke English. Before college she learned Latin. In college, she added American Sign Language, French, German, Italian, and French Sign

Language. She doesn't count lip reading, and, ever modest, is quick to point out that she is not fluent in all seven. As if that matters.

But the most extraordinary thing about Elienne is that she considers her deafness, which 99.9% of the world labels a handicap, to be her greatest asset. "Hearing people should learn how to practice selective deafness, like I do," she says with a laugh. "When someone says no to me, I'm deaf — *of course* I can't hear them! But somehow when someone says yes I always manage to understand."

A deaf empowerment advocate, motivational speaker, and budding author, Elienne believes her message is true for anyone. "There is so much of what we want, and it is all around us," she says. "More love, more money, more chances to help others, more success. Opportunity is everywhere — we just need to open our ears and say yes."

CHAPTER 23

Rising above
Their Circumstances

In case you're not convinced, here are a few examples of people who, though eventually successful, faced some tough times:

- Michael Jordan was cut from his high school basketball team.
- Babe Ruth spent his childhood years in an orphanage and, as a baseball player, struck out 1,330 times, nearly twice as often as he hit his 714 home runs.
- James Earl Jones overcame a serious speech impediment to develop one of the most recognizable voices in the world.
- Major league pitcher Jim Abbott lived his dream of winning in the Major Leagues as a member of the California Angels, New York Yankees, and several other teams (even throwing a no-hitter against the Cleveland Indians) despite being born without a right hand.
- Physicist and best-selling author Stephen Hawking has changed the way the world looks at the structure of the universe, holds the seat at Cambridge University once held by

Sir Isaac Newton, and has been called the greatest cosmological mind since Einstein. This despite being wheelchair bound and unable to speak or move due to Lou Gehrig's Disease.

- Lance Armstrong was a moderately successful professional cyclist when he was diagnosed with testicular cancer in 1996 at age twenty five. His doctors told him the cancer had invaded his brain and that his chance of survival was, at best, 50-50. He recovered not only to ride again, not only to compete again, but to win the Tour de France repeatedly.

- After only one performance, Elvis Presley was banished from the Grand Ole Opry and told, "You ain't goin' nowhere, son."

- Walt Disney was once fired because because he "had no good ideas." He also endured multiple business failures before founding Disneyland.

- George Washington lost two-thirds of all his battles...but he won at Yorktown, and that's the one we remember.

And that's just a very short list of people who overcame obstacles that must have seemed utterly impossible. Start your own list. Who do you know who's done the impossible?

CHAPTER 24

The Real Superman

---

*The hero is one who kindles a great light in the world,
who sets up blazing torches in the dark streets of life for
men to see by.*

— Felix Adler

Many of us are familiar with Christopher Reeve's story. Despite the terrible riding accident that turned him into a quadriplegic, Chris remains positive and motivated. In a huge irony, adversity, courage, hard work, and a giving spirit enabled him to overcome tragedy and go from playing the part of a superhero to becoming one in real life.

Chris obviously learned many important lessons during his formative years. How else could he have found the strength to overcome this dramatic turn of events?

Since his accident, Chris has directed his first movie and returned to acting. His rehab schedule rivals the workouts of some professional athletes. He is a tireless advocate, raising awareness and funding research to cure paralysis caused by spinal cord injury and other central nervous system disorders. He absolutely believes that he will walk again. Listening to him, it is hard to believe anything else.

How many people could continue to lead such a positive and productive life under these circumstances? I can tell you from personal experience that even before his accident, Chris possessed both deep compassion and an understanding of heartbreak.

Several years ago, tragedy struck my family. My nineteen-month-old nephew was killed in a freak accident. The whole family was devastated. At that time, Chris lived in the same town and must have read about the accident in the local paper.

My brother and his wife tried as best they could to console their other son, John. About a week after the funeral, they received a phone call from a stranger who offered to help.

A few hours later, there was a knock at the door. In walked Superman. Chris spent about two hours in John's room, telling stories and trying to lift his spirits. His acting career was booming, but he was not too busy to reach out to a little boy who was grieving and confused. His loving gesture lifted John's spirits and brought the family one step closer to coping with the devastating loss.

Since Chris' own tragic accident, the whole world has had the opportunity to witness his character, courage, and determination — something we were already privileged to know.

Does Chris' life have greater purpose after his accident than it did before? Only he could say for sure. But there is one part of his story that no one can debate: This extraordinary man has turned his hardship into a source of power and purpose that is changing the world.

CHAPTER 25

On Overcoming

Adversity

The first time you quit, it's hard. The second time, it gets easier. The third time, you don't even have to think about it. — Bear Bryant

In the middle of difficulty lies opportunity. — Albert Einstein

It is said an eastern monarch once charged his wise men to invent a sentence, to be ever in view, and which should be true and appropriate in all times and situations. They presented him with the words, "And this, too, shall pass away." — Abraham Lincoln

It takes twenty years to become an overnight success. — Eddie Cantor

Life is not easy for any of us. But what of that? We must have perseverance and, above all, confidence in ourselves. We must believe that we are gifted for something, and that this something, at whatever cost, must be attained. — Marie Curie

A clever man commits no minor blunders. — Wolfgang VonGoethe

Fall seven times, stand up eight. — Japanese Proverb

He conquers who endures. — Perseus

Although the world is full of suffering, it is full also of the overcoming of it. — Helen Keller

People are like stained-glass windows. They sparkle and shine when the sun is out, but when the darkness sets in, their true beauty is revealed only if there is a light from within. — Elizabeth Kübler-Ross

Effort only fully releases its reward after a person refuses to quit. — Napoleon Hill

Conquering any difficulty always gives one a secret joy, for it means pushing back a boundary-line and adding to one's liberty. — Henri Frederic Amiel

Adversity is the first path to truth. — George Gordon Byron

In this age, which believes that there is a short cut to everything, the greatest lesson to be learned is that the most difficult way is, in the long run, the easiest. — Henry Miller

PART THREE

FOUNDATION #2

WORK HARD

CHAPTER 26

The "Secret" to Success

Whatever your hand finds to do, do it with all your might.

— Ecclesiastes 9:10

She routinely works fourteen hours a day, has more than one job, and has to get up early to squeeze in personal time. Who is she? A student putting herself through school? A single mother struggling to keep her family housed and fed? No. She's one of the world's wealthiest women.

Oprah Winfrey writes, reads, produces, acts, maintains a public speaking schedule, and works out. She owns a production studio, publishes a magazine, started a book club, travels extensively, is an active philanthropist, and is reported to personally sign all the checks that are written for her businesses. Oh, and she also hosts two daily television shows.

Why Would Anybody *Do* That?

Oprah and people like her know a secret that many people never push themselves hard enough to find out. They have come to know work as a "how" not a "what." They have discovered that human beings are built to achieve and to excel.

This is not new information. "We are what we repeatedly do. Excellence, then, is not an act but a habit," Aristotle taught. Human beings take more pleasure in something as we become more proficient at it. We enjoy using our capacities to the fullest. It makes sense that a skill earned with hard work would bring us the most pleasure of all.

Centuries later, Abraham Maslow shook the science of human psychology in two ways. He boldly theorized that once basic needs were met, human beings would strive for higher things. This is Maslow's famous "Hierarchy of Needs." In this theory, humans who had satisfied their basic survival requirements would then turn to self-actualization in art, scientific exploration, public service, or problem solving. Maslow's examples of people who achieved self-actualization reads like a *Who's Who* of humanity: Albert Einstein, Abraham Lincoln, Eleanor Roosevelt, and Thomas Jefferson, to name a few.

Perhaps humans are hardwired to pursue excellence.

Everything's Better When You Earn It

Although there are people who can't conceive of work as its own reward, the idea makes a lot of sense. Have you ever noticed that a cold, frosted glass of ice water tastes much more satisfying after

"Success is the sum of small efforts, *repeated day in and day out."*

— Robert Collier

mowing the lawn or finishing a good run. Why? It's exactly the same water that's available to you the rest of the time. But that one is special because you earned it.

Or in high school, each of us had a different favorite subject, but there's no denying that an A in Algebra or Organic Chemistry felt like a much bigger deal the same grade in Music or Phys Ed! When it comes to establishing a grade point average one A is as good as another, but students everywhere place a premium on the grades they sweat for.

If You Love It, It's Not Work

Then there's my friend, Penny: wife, mother, accountant, and business manager. I know her as an author. Every day, she gets up and writes for at least an hour, before the rest of her family starts the day. People who are "too tired" before and after work are people who don't know what they love. Not having passion is exhausting.

Ask the thousands of artisans around the world who make a modest living working to create beautiful handmade sweaters, furniture, fishing rods, and the like. None of these activities is necessarily high paying. But those who are driven by a passion to create tell us that the joy and satisfaction their work provides are worth infinitely more than money. Such people are truly rich.

As Oprah has said, "You know you are on the road to success if you would do your job and not be paid for it." She went on to say that she would do her job and "take on a second job to make ends meet...just for the opportunity to do it. That's how you know you are doing the right thing."

Can Work Really Be Its Own Reward?

Still not convinced? The late Mother Teresa spent decades caring for the poorest of human beings in the filthiest, most wretched conditions in Calcutta. One day, a person conducting an interview with her commented, "You couldn't pay me enough to do what you do." Her reply? "Me either."

Work well done yields self-esteem. Real self-esteem depends, in part, on the knowledge that we can take care of ourselves and accomplish what needs to be done. Kids who can feel good about a neatly weeded garden or a well-made bed don't have to wait for someone else to come along and "validate" them. They have learned that their own efforts produce results.

Everybody works at something, although as author Richard Bach said, "The more I want to get something done, the less I call it work." When our kids are young, we have the opportunity to introduce them to the attitudes and ethics that will follow them throughout their working lives. Those who are able to approach their work with enthusiasm, joy, and a desire for excellence have received a priceless gift: the ability to enjoy all seven days of every week!

CHAPTER 27

Good Work Habits

Begin Early

Your grandparents had a different word for burger flipping. They called it opportunity.

— Charles J. Sykes

My father's mentor and business partner, Tony Cersosimo, picked tobacco in his youth. Tony's son Butch picked up sticks in the lumber yard for fifteen cents an hour. My brother painted miles of fences, and I worked as a chambermaid. My son and my nephew caddied, stacked wood, and unloaded hay. We were fortunate. We learned how to work.

Every successful person we interviewed for this book worked as a child. They had responsibilities both inside and outside the home. Children need to play and to study, but if they don't develop a work ethic and good habits while they are young, how and when do we expect them to learn these things? Responsibility and self-sufficiency take time to develop.

Working Kids Learn about Value

While some high-flying adults were motivated by childhood deprivation, others learned from parents who were wonderful examples. Bonnie Koenig is a dynamic and astute private banker. She grew up in a small town in Michigan, the fourth of seven children. Being a middle child taught her the value of teamwork. As part of a large family with a modest income, she learned the value of hard work. She has applied both those lessons to her advantage in the corporate world.

"When I was younger, I was embarrassed because I had to work on Saturdays when my friends could go play," she says. "I started with babysitting jobs. At sixteen, I had a summer job at the root beer stand. There were so few jobs for kids that having a chance to work was a privilege. In high school, I entered a co-op program that placed students in the community for a half day of work. I got to work at the city newspaper."

Every afternoon, Bonnie went to the police and fire stations to collect information to write her articles. She also covered the high school news. "I had a column in the *Daily Press* with my own byline," she says. "The summer after high school, I worked three jobs. I went to the paper in the morning, ran a 'tot lot' for sixty kids for a few hours, and waitressed at night."

All that work didn't mean her parents gave her a break from household chores; she had those, too. Her parents knew that when kids contribute to the household by doing chores, they learn important life skills and develop stronger family bonds. And with seven children, they needed the help.

Kids who work and do chores learn to value the efforts of others...and find out firsthand that families need to pull together to accomplish their goals.

CHAPTER 28

What Do You Want?

Imagination is more important than knowledge.

— Albert Einstein

If you don't have a destination in mind, how will you know when you get there? Going through life without goals is like meandering around on country roads. It's pleasant and relaxing, but at the end of the day, where are you? And while that's fine for a Sunday afternoon when you don't care where you end up, our lives are another matter.

Whether you want to lose weight, buy a new bike, or end illiteracy around the world, you can't set a goal — and certainly can't reach it — unless you first have the desire to make something happen. You have to want something.

Don't Fulfill Every Want

Success stories begin with a dream, grow with goal-setting, and are fueled by persistent action. Parents who satisfy a child's every want deprive that child of something he or she really needs: the experience of lacking something long enough to figure out how to do something about it!

In our interviews, many successful people identified early wants that guided their life choices. Dad's mentor, Tony, wanted to "amount to something" and to ride in an airplane. Dave Thomas desperately wanted a Cadillac.

Mark Victor Hansen tells a similar story. At the age of nine, his heart's great desire was to own a very expensive racing bike. Once he got his dad's permission to buy it with his own money, Mark caught fire and sold greeting cards door to door until he had earned enough to buy his bike.

Sometimes children dream about things that are impossible for them to attain. Dad's dream of pitching in a World Series game never came true, but Grampa Pat never discouraged that dream. Instead, when Dad wanted the baseball glove that would make him the next Cy Young, Grampa Pat helped him figure out how to earn the money. My father never made it to Major League Baseball, but he learned the sales skills that have taken him to the big leagues in his career.

It All Starts with Desire

Did Dad or Mark want to be the top nine-year-old salesmen in their neighborhoods? No. Dad wanted a baseball glove, and Mark wanted a bike. Their wants motivated them to work to acquire their desires. They learned some important life skills along the way.

To strike out in search of bigger opportunities, or to buy something special without burdening hardworking parents — before every goal comes a want that is unfulfilled. Wanting moves us to act. All successful people start out with desires and goals. Desire lights the fuse of vision — the ability to see what we truly can be.

CHAPTER 29

Does Hard

Work Pay Off?

Lord, grant that I may always desire more than I can accomplish.

— Michelangelo

Ask these people if their hard work paid off:

- Wayne Gretzky tried out for pro hockey and was told, "You don't weigh enough. You won't be able to survive on the rink."
- Bill Porter was a legend in door-to-door sales despite being born with cerebral palsy.
- Liz Murray is the daughter of drug-addicted parents. She finished high school in two years and got into Harvard University. She often did her homework while sitting in the stairwell of her school and did not share the fact that she was homeless, because she feared being placed in foster care. Her story was told in the movie *Homeless to Harvard*.

- Country singer Shania Twain grew up in a Canadian mining town. Her father abandoned the family when she was a toddler. As a young child, she planted trees with her stepfather as part of a forestry crew. When her parents were killed in an accident when she was twenty two, Shania set aside her musical aspirations to become the legal guardian of her two half brothers and her sister.

- Erin Brockovich, a crusader for the "little guy" who became the subject of an Oscar-winning film, was an unemployed mother of three with no prospects, a broken collarbone, and a mountain of medical debt when she talked lawyer Ed Masry into hiring her as a file clerk.

- Whoopi Goldberg worked as a bricklayer and funeral home cosmetician.

- Cosmetics queen Mary Kay Ash cared for an invalid father while her mother worked, then spent twenty five years as a saleswoman before starting the company that would make her famous.

- Wally Amos worked to build one successful cookie company, lost control of it, then built another...and another....

- Country music legend Johnny Cash supported his family by plowing fields, picking cotton, and hunting for game to put on the table. Later he would sell appliances door to door.

CHAPTER 30

The Role Model
of a Lifetime

D ad's early professional life was full of gifts and lessons that expanded upon his childhood training. Among them was a relationship with a man whose character and experience reflect all the principles in this book.

When Dad decided to go into business for himself, he need-ed to locate and purchase a large tract of land. He scoured the classifieds, talked to local realtors and studied tax maps in count-less small towns. Finally, he found it — five hundred gorgeous acres in a small village in southern Vermont. It was perfect.

But there was a problem. His modest savings would have made a nice down payment, but banks did not give loans on undeveloped land. Dad needed help. He remembered a name he had encountered repeatedly in his search. Tony Cersosimo was a lumberman who owned a great deal of land, but did not wish to sell any of it. So Dad decided to approach Tony to ask him to finance the project.

Tony didn't exactly greet Dad and his proposal with enthusiasm; he needed "time to think it over." Dad took this time-honored phrase to mean "Thanks but no thanks."

But Tony was a man of his word. He really did need time to think it over. A few days later he showed up, check in hand, saying, "I'm here to be your partner." Dad was ecstatic. At 32, he was on his way to his first big land deal. But he had no idea how much this partnership would change and influence his life.

Taking Pride in Their Work

Tony Cersosimo was one of nine children born to Italian parents who migrated to America to make a better life. "In the old country, my father's father and other men in the family traveled from town to town, cutting trees with a broad ax and curing them into timbers that people used for their homes," he said. "And at night they played the guitar and sang and danced — and the women in all the towns waited for them, so I heard. But I didn't want to cut wood all my life."

Tony grew up on a farm in East Hartford, Connecticut, and earned $1.10 a day picking tobacco leaves. At home, the family raised their own vegetables, pigs, and cattle.

"The entire family worked on the farm," says Tony. "We were pretty good workers, so we also hired out as a team to take in other people's crops and butcher their hogs or cattle for them. I used to brag about how much hay we could pitch and how much wood we could cut."

Learning to Work Made Everything Possible

Tony described the impact of his early work experience. "When I was a kid I often heard my mother use the phrase 'amount to something.' I wasn't completely sure what that was, but it made me want to try," he said. "But there was no money for college and no school loans back then."

So when "a lady came to the farm selling the idea of business school," he borrowed five dollars from a friend, enrolled, and started working in a restaurant. "I made the Dean's List right away... with hardly any sleep," he says, "since I was working eight hours a day plus doing my homework. I graduated in two years."

"The only honest measure of your success is what you are doing compared to your true potential."

— Paul J. Meyer

Despite landing a good job working for a lumber company in Vermont during World War II, Tony yearned to go into business for himself. "You never get anywhere working for someone else — you have to do it for yourself," he said. "I wanted to make a lot of money and to be in a position where I could help other people, particularly kids."

The business Tony founded became one of the largest lumber companies in the Northeast. He surpassed the goals he had set for himself and touched the lives of countless people. Although Tony came from humble beginnings, his parents provided him with everything he needed to succeed in life — things money could not buy.

A True Success

Tony was eighty six years old when died in 2002. A few days after his passing, Sean McKeon, the Executive Director of the Northeast Regional Forest Foundation, spoke about the impact of Tony's life, calling him "a man who was a success in the most complete sense of the word."

McKeon said this of Tony and his life's work:

"Companies that utilize natural resources have had to grow and change with the times, and his company was always on the cutting edge. Yet Tony's legacy is far more than a sophisticated and profitable business empire. There are many whose lives Tony touched in a profound way, individuals who knew him as more than a successful business leader or powerful member of the community. In many respects, the lumber industry reflects the traditional values that marked Tony's life: hard work and dedication, loyalty and a commitment to excellence, and a love for a way of life that is perhaps gone forever. Tony achieved beyond any expectations. His wisdom was simple: Work hard and concentrate on what you do best. I'm glad I had the chance to meet him."

Most of us don't have the chance to grow up on a family farm where survival demands teamwork. However, all families have tasks that must be completed to keep the family unit running smoothly. It's easier to take out the trash yourself than to teach your child to be responsible for it. But there's much more than trash at stake.

CHAPTER 31

That Competitive Fire

It's about striving for excellence, going after something true and noble... fair play and sportsmanship... being the best that you can be... commitment, persistence, discipline, vision, and focus. The ultimate triumph is in the journey, not just the destination...it's the striving, not just the winning, that makes a great Olympian.

— Bob Costas

"Try your hardest." "Do your best." "Practice." "Be on time." Whether it was a spelling bee, a ski race, or band competition, these are the values and ideas associated with competition, at least when my dad was growing up. How has something that can offer so many benefits become so controversial?

Winning takes effort, determination, focus, and desire. Children can learn important lessons about commitment, self-confidence, and teamwork. Losing can teach grace, perseverance, and the ability to rebound from defeat. Winning and losing are still some of the best teachers around. Competition drives us to reach our potential, shows us what it takes to reach the highest levels, and often shows us we're capable of more than we thought. Most high achievers thrive on competition.

Depends on the Source

Of course, the benefits depend on where the competitive pressure comes from. "Competition can be a very intense experience and a very rewarding one, or it can be enormously destructive," said former Olympic ski racer and medalist Andrea Mead Lawrence. "External pressure, whether it's exerted by a coach, a school, a ski club, or a country can make it a negative thing. When they use you to satisfy their need to succeed, when they impose their value system on you, then competition isn't personally rewarding anymore."

Don Dion recalls his first experience with competition. "Fourth grade was the first year you could try out for the hockey team," he says. "Twenty kids tried out; five made it. The results were posted on the board at school. That was the start of winning and losing. I didn't make the team and felt really horrible. Sometimes you lose. You have to deal with it and plan so that it doesn't happen again."

Competitiveness Is Just Another Life Skill

It's easy to find articles about adults who bring cutthroat mentalities and even violence to youth sports. That's not competition. Smart parents recognize healthy competition as a fact of life, and that it can be a useful part of preparing a child to survive and excel.

"Playing a sport can help kids stay out of trouble and build self-confidence," said the late Arthur Ashe. "You learn to fend for yourself, and when things get very rough and you cannot lean on anybody else's second opinion, we're going to find out if you've got any character."

Don't Protect Kids from Competition

Some parents make the mistake of trying to shield their children from competition, unaware that they're sending a dangerous message: "You don't have to compete. You are entitled." In a sense, parents who protect their children from the "dangers" of competing are exercising a kind of economic elitism.

"To dream anything that you want to dream, that is the beauty of the human mind. To do anything that you want to do, that is the strength of the human will. To trust yourself, to test your limits, that is the courage to succeed."

— Bernard Edmonds

They're saying, "I have the financial means to erect a barrier around my child." But what happens when those parents are not around?

An intention that may have begun as an expression of unconditional love instead burdens kids with yet another attitude that will make it more difficult for them to succeed as adults.

There are other parents who, because of the lessons learned during their financial struggles, would never consider doing such a thing, even if they could. Parents who have triumphed over their own struggles know competition isn't fatal, and if kids don't learn to compete, they learn to quit.

We Are Our Own Best Opponent

Competition cannot teach kids that they'll always win if they work hard. They may learn that coaches and referees are not always fair. The same is true for life. Children who learn this lesson early understand that they are entitled to nothing — that to get what they want, they must outwork everyone else.

Competition's greatest lessons take time to uncover. A kid who has learned to compete can look forward to the joy that comes from performing at her best. Top achievers learn two important lessons:

1. Their real opponents are their own limits and fears.
2. Those who don't compete don't lose, but they also can't win.

Competitiveness is an essential life skill. Whether it's positive or negative depends on what you and your children decide to do with it.

CHAPTER 32

Junior Achievement

Habits are formed in youth...what we need in this country now...is to teach the growing generations to realize that thrift and economy, coupled with industry, are as necessary now as they were in past generations.

— Theodore Vail

Imagine a world in which first- and second-graders debate the relative merits of renting mall space to a candy store or a veterinarian's office. Or where middle schoolers read stock quotes and high school students not only run the school store — they *own* it. Is this some kind of weird fantasy? No. It's Junior Achievement, and it's probably in your community.

Junior Achievement (or JA) is a group of passionate adults who seek to inspire kids to improve the quality of their lives through mastery of the free enterprise system.

It's a partnership between young people, their schools, and the business community. Adult volunteers share their experience with students, introducing concepts and skills that they will need in the world of work.

Origins

In 1919, Strathmore Paper Company founder Horace Moses and two colleagues, Theodore Vail (president of American Telephone and Telegraph) and Senator Murray Crane, founded JA in Western Massachusetts. They hoped that kids in urban areas would benefit from experiential education — like 4-H for their rural peers.

They were also concerned about the lack of a trained work force and felt that, unless students were introduced to the concepts of a free market economy early in life, they could never reach their full potential within that system. They used the Eastern States Exposition, New England's largest regional fair, to introduce the new organization.

They described its purpose as "to interest boys and girls in productive work, giving them an appreciation of the earned dollar, an understanding of the opportunity and dignity of honest labor and the joy of success." Moses hoped that experience in JA would provide young people with both sound work ethics and marketable skills.

In less than a century, JA has grown to become an international organization, involving more than six million students in its sequential programming each year. It's not difficult to help bring this valuable learning experience to your child's classroom, and there are many ways you can support JA in your community: attend its events, provide job shadow opportunities, serve on a board, or become a classroom volunteer.

JA offers us all a simple way to work with our schools to improve financial literacy skills in our communities.

CHAPTER 33

It's Never

Too Early to Be

Entrepreneurial

Innovation is the specific instrument of entrepreneurship... the act that endows resources with a new capacity to create wealth.

— Peter F. Drucker

Not long ago, most workers could step into a lifetime job with regular pay raises, promotions, and a good pension at retirement. Our economy has changed. Those days are gone. To survive in today's job market, workers have to shoulder more responsibility for their careers.

To move ahead, most will have to understand the entire business, not just their own jobs. Nothing can provide a more solid foundation for young adults entering the workforce than entrepreneurial experience in their formative years.

Entrepreneurs Aren't Just Business Owners

Being entrepreneurial means more than running a small business. The artist must sell her work. The lawyer must obtain new clients. The grant writer must sell his concept. Early entrepreneurial experiences can prepare kids to excel in many ways.

Most of the people Dad and I interviewed for this book ran small businesses in childhood. Paper routes, lawn mowing, snow shoveling, babysitting, door-to-door sales, shoeshine boxes, and lemonade stands — those were just some of the ways enterpris-

"Really it comes down to your philosophy. Do you want to be safe and good, or do you want to take a chance and be great?"

— Jimmy Johnson

ing kids learned to make money and develop their business skills. Golfers are familiar with the young tycoons who scavenge stray balls to resell — and Dad buys them every chance he gets.

These business experiences are fertile ground for developing a good work ethic and self-discipline. Kids also learn that their earning power is proportionate to their effort, and that earning money gives them the opportunity to influence their circumstances.

Kids with something to sell and a compelling reason to sell it quickly learn to make eye contact and speak clearly. Words like *please, thank you, sir*, and *ma'am* turn up in their vocabularies. The confidence and self-sufficiency that come from developing business and sales skills early in life open lots of doors.

CHAPTER 34

Charlie and Dixie

---

*One hundred percent of the shots you
don't take don't go in.*

— Wayne Gretzky

Charlie and Dixie Patterson are dynamic and upbeat.
Married for more than forty years, they have developed a
thriving business and a happy, healthy family. They have divided
those jobs along traditional lines. Dixie has assumed most of the
responsibility "on the home front" and Charlie is the breadwin-
ner, but to anyone who knows them, there's no doubt that they
are a team. Their life together is built on the Four Foundations,
and they have passed many important lessons on to their children.

Charlie grew up in his parents' bakery. His earliest days were
spent napping on a doughnut-mixing machine while his parents
worked. Dixie's father died young, and her mother brought up
five girls on her own. Is it surprising that their personal work
ethics blossomed early?

"My dad got up at three o'clock in the morning to go to work, six days a week," Charlie says. "My mother worked in the bakery, too. And they were very ethical. They treated the employees right. My dad owned it, started it, made it bigger, moved to a better location, and made it a success. So I saw what hard work will do. That's why I always wanted to work in my own business."

A Young Businessman

Charlie's entrepreneurial urge kicked in when he was very young. "At about eight, I had a shoeshine stand on the corner," he recalls. "Most of the time I got everybody's socks black instead of their shoes. I had lemonade stands and sold papers. And I always worked in the bakery."

When he got older, Charlie was one of the few kids in his high school to have his own car. It was the station wagon that he bought to use delivering doughnuts from his Dad's shop to all the local schools — before leaving to start his own school day. "It may not have been the coolest car I could have had but I bought it, and it was all mine," he says.

Early entrepreneurial experiences teach children valuable lessons, not only about making a living, but also about their inner strength, creativity, and independence. Listen closely. What kinds of businesses are your kids itching to start?

CHAPTER 35

Nearly 100, Work Keeps Him Young

Arthur Winston started cleaning trolley cars for the Los Angeles Railway Company in 1924, when he was just seventeen. He quit for a while, but returned to work in 1934 and has been going strong for 70 years — and in all that time, has missed only a single day of work, when his wife died in 1988.

Punching the Clock Every Day

Winston doesn't make a big deal out of his dedication. It is his job to show up every day and do his best. According to his records, he has never arrived late, never left early, and always done a first-rate job. In the process, he's become a local legend and an amazing example of the restorative, healthful power of work.

A healthy, slender African-American man with a slow but steady walk, he seems never to be ill. He keeps moving to stay warm on cold mornings, and it's hard to find him standing still at any time on the job; he'd rather hop into a bus and start scrubbing the floors or cleaning up discarded gum. He lives on his own in South Los Angeles, where everyone seems to know him.

The Power of Purpose

Characteristically humble, Winston wouldn't call his work important. But the lesson he lives is priceless: a steady dedication to a job well done is its own reward. His job continues to give him purpose, a place to go, and a sense that he is giving back to his community. Work keeps Arthur Winston young, even at the age of ninety seven.

In seven decades of making trolleys and buses more pleasant for the people of L.A., Winston has come up with a few bits of "working man" wisdom (courtesy of the *Los Angeles Times*):

- Working men are simple and humble.
- They use their money wisely.
- They arrive fifteen minutes before their shift starts.
- They keep their uniforms crisp.
- They do not fuss, mope, or complain.

A Tribute

Winston's simple wisdom has helped him thrive during a working life that's been twice as long as most people's. If you make it to L.A., look him up and share a good word with him. You'll find him where he always is: going to work every morning at what's been renamed the Arthur Winston Bus Division, off 54th Street and Van Ness Avenue. If you never make it, remember the example he's set. Simple, honest work done well can be more than character-building and financially rewarding. It can be noble.

CHAPTER 36

On Hard Work

Your paycheck is not your employer's responsibility. It's your responsibility. Your employer has no control over your value, but you do.
— Jim Rohn

If you have a job without aggravations, you don't have a job.
— Malcolm S. Forbes

I am a strong believer in luck, and I find the harder I work the more I have of it.
— Benjamin Franklin

It has been my experience that one cannot, in any shape or form, depend on human relations for lasting reward. It is only work that truly satisfies.
— Bette Davis

Real success is finding your lifework in the work that you love.
— David McCullough

Find a job you like and you add five days to every week.
— H. Jackson Brown, Jr.

To find out what one is fitted to do, and to secure an opportunity to do it, is the key to happiness. — John Dewey

Hard work spotlights the character of people: some turn up their sleeves, some turn up their noses, and some don't turn up at all. — Sam Ewig

Work is love made visible. And if you cannot work with love but only with distaste, it is better that you should leave your work and sit at the gate of the temple and take alms of those who work with joy. — Kahlil Gibran

The secret of joy in work is contained in one word — excellence. To know how to do something well is to enjoy it. — Pearl Buck

Intelligence without ambition is a bird without wings. — C. Archie Danielson

We cannot restore integrity and morality to our society until each of us — singly and individually — takes responsibility for our actions. — Harry Emerson Fosdick

Real excellence and humility are not incompatible with the other, on the contrary they are twin sisters. — Jean Baptiste Lacordaire

We have to do the best we can. This is our sacred human responsibility." — Albert Einstein

Be ashamed to die unless you have won some victory for humanity. — Horace Mann

PART FOUR

FOUNDATION #3
DEVELOP DISCIPLINE

CHAPTER *37*

Cut That Out,

Right NOW!

The goal of parental discipline should be the achievement of the child's self-discipline, not parental control of the child's behavior.

— Janice Presser

Have you ever wondered why some parents can settle an entire carload of eight-year-olds with a single eyeball in the rearview mirror while others seem unable to enforce a simple time-out? Perhaps one knows that children want to live up to their parents' high standards, while the other wants to be the "good guy" and get the approval of her child.

Discipline seems to have become confused with punishment. Kids without discipline are left on their own to figure out socially acceptable behavior. It's a form of abandonment.

Does this sound familiar? "Children these days are tyrants. They not only talk back to their parents, teachers, and elders, but they expect every luxury, gobble their food, chatter incessantly, and sneer at any attempt to control them." If that sounds like the rant of a parent on a talk show, it's not. It was Socrates in the 5th century, BC. Shaping child behavior has been an issue for millennia.

Expectations Are Clear

Every generation thinks the generations that follow are setting new standards for bad behavior. But I'm not sure bullying, cruel behavior, and violence are matters of opinion. They're sad facts. Why are children not being taught what is acceptable behavior?

When my father was a boy and he crossed over the well-defined boundaries of proper behavior, what bothered him most was that he had disappointed his parents. Stealing, vandalism, and violence were not even discussed. They didn't need to be.

Dad's parents never explicitly laid out "The Rules," but their expectations were crystal clear. Honesty and hard work were givens, as were fair dealing and good sportsmanship. So were being polite, respectful, and helpful to all elders, all the time.

Dad talks about what happened when he crossed the line: "There were consequences. Privileges were taken away or additional chores were added to teach me a lesson and to enforce standards," he says. "I'm sure I complained, but I always knew that the uncomfortable feelings I was experiencing were brought about by my own behavior — and that I alone could determine the length of time until my next trip to the doghouse."

Tasks and Attention to Detail

The adult achievers Dad and I interviewed all told us they had strong role models who established clear, non-negotiable boundaries. Remember Bonnie Koenig, the executive banker? She credits her parents with giving her the discipline and structure she needed to accomplish any task.

"I am highly organized and know how to finish a task," Bonnie says. "I learned these skills when I was very young. During the week, we cleaned up the table or rinsed, washed, or dried the dishes. We cleaned the mudroom and made sure all the little kids' boots and coats were dry and put away. We all drew for family jobs on Saturday mornings, and one of the jobs I inevitably got was vacuuming. My dad always inspected afterwards. One of his favorite pieces of advice was, 'Take care of the corners, and the rest will take care of itself.' Every time he said that I'd cringe. The message was 'If you take care of the details, the big part is easy.'"

Getting the Job Done

Today, Bonnie's associates comment on her attention to detail. "Some people think that when you get to a client's detail work, you can delegate it to someone else or just let it slide," she says. "But I find that if you do one small job very thoroughly for your clients, they will give you a second and a third. Too many people in the business world want to 'hit the high points' and don't want to do the rest. I learned to 'take care of the corners' as a child. It's automatic as an adult."

The childhood homes of successful adults had structure that taught standards and set boundaries. They honored and obeyed their parents and other adults in their community. Back talk was simply not an option. My sister-in-law Cindy put it this way:

"My job is to raise a competent adult, not to be my son's friend. He's got plenty of friends. I have to set a good example."

"It was very important when I was a kid, to respect older people and to respect the rules," adds Don Dion. "The teacher was always right. If you did something wrong, your parents automatically agreed with the teacher. They didn't ask for your 'vote' on it."

Discipline Isn't Difficult

Developing discipline need not be overwhelming. It can start with the teaching of manners — waiting until Mom or Dad is finished talking, or saying *please* and *thank you* without being prompted. It can be expanded to include the assignment of simple daily chores such as setting the dinner table, taking out the trash, or shoveling the walk. These behaviors and tasks can yield valuable lessons: the ability to delay gratification, the importance of good work habits, how to see an assignment through to its conclusion, and improvement through daily repetition.

A business owner I know, who raised her children as a single parent, says, "When I first started work, my kids never even knew it. Throughout their grammar school years, I left the house when they got on the school bus and I got home when they did. If they arrived home before me, they didn't watch TV. I left them a list of chores on the kitchen counter. They knew the chores had to be completed or there would be a consequence.

"I started working full-time when my youngest was in high school," she continues. "At that point, my kids had formed their own values and I could focus on my career. I have never had to worry about them. They knew right from wrong."

Discipline becomes a way of life.

CHAPTER 38

Charlotte Meets
the 28 Rules

This beauty pageant was unique. Most of the audience was thinking about the clothes and hairstyles of the girls on the stage. But a few people were thinking about a diaper-clad little kid who had stood unsupervised in the New England cold — a dirty, underfed little girl whose hair fell out in clumps while her mother stood on the street corner arguing with someone no one else could see.

They were thinking about that former foster child, and delighting in the fact that no one in that audience could pick that girl out from among the other teen beauties standing center stage.

A Rebellious Kid

Charlotte spent the first three years of her life living in the neglect and squalor that was all her severely mentally ill mother could provide. Calls from concerned neighbors brought police, who removed Charlotte and her siblings and placed them in temporary foster care.

Going to live with strangers can be traumatic, but in many cases, foster care saves lives. In this case, it may have done exactly that. However, having a state for a parent can also exaggerate feelings of isolation and rejection leading some kids to feel like permanent outsiders. By the time Charlotte was a teen, still not adopted by her long-term foster family, she was hurt, resentful, and rebellious. Her angry behavior landed her in a new foster home...with a list of twenty eight not-to-be-broken rules:

House Rules

1. *All issues will be honestly and openly discussed. Lies will result in loss of night or nights out.*

2. *Stealing will not be tolerated. Inventory will be taken on arrival and when you leave.*

3. *Articles which are not your own personal possessions are not to be taken from this house.*

4. *When I am not home, no one is allowed to enter the house except those who live here. Permission must be given by me for friends to come and visit. Visits during evening hours will be limited. Exception: caseworkers.*

5. *No drugs and alcohol in and around the house. I will keep and dispense all medication.*

6. *Anyone who comes home stoned or drunk will be grounded for one month.*

7. *No long distance calls unless permission is given and arrangements have been made to pay for the call(s).*

8. *No incoming or outgoing calls before 9:00 a.m. or after 9:00 p.m. No fighting or arguing on the phone. Timer must be set for ten minutes and permission given to use the phone.*

9. *Respect to all members of the household is necessary for a happy*

and harmonious home; therefore, all complaints must be discussed and worked out through a family meeting whenever someone feels it is necessary.

10. Nights out require two days' previous notice. During the week (Sunday through Thursday) age 14 and up, 10:00 p.m. curfew.

11. Lateness will be dealt with according to: time, reason, condition you come home in and frequency. Grounding could result.

12. Everyone is expected to be home for dinner (5:30 – 6:30) unless special arrangements have been made. Kitchen closes at 7:00 p.m.

13. Grades must be maintained at a reasonable level — C. Any failure or dips in grades will result in fewer nights out. Improvements in grades will be rewarded with your choice of money or an extra night out every other week — your choice. $3 for A's, $1 for B's.

14. Bedtime is 10:00 p.m. Sunday through Thursday. Lights out is at your discretion. If you are sharing a room it becomes a mutual agreement. If an agreement cannot be reached I will help.

15. I am always available to talk, if you need help or just want to talk. This home is open to all subjects of discussion.

16. Unless you display behavior which is inappropriate, you will be treated as a responsible young adult. (This means controlling yourself in public places or you will not be in public places.)

17. No form of verbal or physical abuse will be tolerated in this home. Anger will be discussed in a civil manner with respect for all feelings involved rather than to say things we do not mean in anger and hurt the feelings of others.

18. Keep your room clean and neat. Beds must be made every day. No exceptions. $5 fine for violations.

19. Smoking is not allowed in the house — ever. Anyone found smoking will lose one week out.

20. *All therapy sessions must be attended.*

21. *Cutting school is not allowed. I will allow occasional days off based on grades and general behavior both inside and outside the house.*

22. *Everyone (except Mom) takes a turn doing dishes and vacuuming.*

23. *You are expected to clean up after yourself. We are all too busy to clean up someone else's mess.*

24. *Due to problems which have arisen, wearing articles of clothing or shoes which are not your own is not permitted. If your clothing allowance is spent wisely, in time you will have plenty of clothes. If clothing is not appropriate, you may not wear it! I determine that.*

25. *No swearing in or around this house. Swearing will result in 1 hour off of your next night out.*

26. *Drive-in movies, rock concerts, amusement parks, malls, out-of-town day trips: age 17 and up. Exceptions can be made at my discretion for all ages.*

27. *You will consistently and correctly report your whereabouts at all times.*

28. *Seven-day orientation for all incomers.*

Definition of grounding: Loss of all privileges, home within one hour of leaving school. Exception: job. No phone calls in or out.

Life under "The Rules"

Does that seem excessive? Prison-like, perhaps? Charlotte would not be the first — or the last — teen to refer to her new foster mom as "the warden." But having worked with kids in Janet Henry's home on many different occasions, I know that Rule #15 made all the others worth obeying. In her years as a foster parent,

Janet's rules were a life raft for lots of kids, and they reflected a number of important principles: everyone here matters, work and school are important, you can and will be responsible, improvement is possible and guess who's responsible for all of that?

So, in a setting of benevolent chaos, this frustrated young girl learned how to set goals and work to achieve them. Her grades improved, she got a job and became a member of her school's track team.

For years, Charlotte sustained herself with dreams of becoming a star. At almost every opportunity, she sang and danced and acted — with an audience at church or alone in her room. It didn't matter. In her mind, she was center stage, under the hot lights, applauded by an enthusiastic audience.

Dreaming of a Family

But deep down, Charlotte always felt temporary. When she looked at the years ahead, there was no place to go on college vacations and no place she "had to be" for Thanksgiving. Even in her midteens, Charlotte still wanted to be adopted. She also still held on to her dream of being a performer. The odds of either were long.

Then one day, opportunity knocked. Sitting at foster mom Janet's dining room table, reading the local paper, Charlotte spotted an ad seeking teens to participate in a regional beauty pageant. She casually mentioned it. Janet, who is anything but casual when it comes to supporting kids and their dreams, said, "Call."

By this time Charlotte had become an attractive, poised, self-confident young woman. She entered the regional pageant...and won, as Janet sat in the audience practically bursting with pride. And as dramatic as that was, there was another drama unfolding behind the scenes. During the months leading up to the Miss Teen USA contest, Charlotte had left Janet's home to practice living with the couple who wanted to adopt her. These were the people who wanted her to come home for Thanksgiving every year.

Only the Beginning

After all that, it was almost anticlimactic that Charlotte became Miss Teen USA 1993. But true to the woman she had become, she didn't stop there. Her achievement awoke a passion she didn't know she had. Charlotte became an advocate for foster kids around the country. She has also been reunited with her brother and built a thriving career as an actress, where she's known as Charlotte Ayanna.

So, by age eighteen, Charlotte had achieved two enormous goals and turned her life into a story of triumph. Strict rules and discipline had helped her realize her true potential. How does that fit your definition of success?

CHAPTER 39

A is for Attitude

It's kind of fun to do the impossible.

— Walt Disney

What is "attitude"? It's a collection of values, beliefs, thoughts, and feelings that direct behavior. It affects the way we present ourselves to the world, tackle new challenges, and treat others. Attitude matters.

A good attitude surfaces in a variety of ways: a great smile, a desire to reach out to people, friendliness, fair-dealing, enthusiasm, integrity. It can include a desire for excellence, extra attention to detail or the willingness to take responsibility. These characteristics may manifest differently in a college classroom than on the floor of the stock exchange, but they are always present in high achievers.

When Dad and I first met Jerome, he owned and managed a lovely inn that served as home base for his work as an independent fishing guide. His warmth, enthusiasm, and attention to detail quickly convinced us that he had a wonderful story to tell.

Defying the Islander Anti-Work Ethic

Jerome grew up in a sleepy St. Lawrence River town in the Thousand Islands region of New York, a summer getaway place for wealthy folks from the city. Generation after generation of locals (also known as "islanders") served the well-to-do visitors until changes in vacation habits took most of their business elsewhere. Over the years both the buildings and the spirit of the community deteriorated. A summer paradise faded to gray and

Meditate.

Live purely. Be quiet.
Do your work with mastery.
Like the moon, come out
from behind the clouds!
Shine.

— Buddha

bleak, both in weather and outlook, over the long, harsh winters.

Jerome grew up surrounded by hard work: his father worked as a fishing guide for a wealthy drug-company owner, and his mother used a big mangle roller washer to do linens for the owners of the visiting yachts.

"My older brothers all went to college," he says. "One went to Annapolis, the hard way, without a congressional appointment. The other graduated from Cornell and became a research scientist there. The whole family shared the goal of creating a better life, and we all started by getting to work at an early age."

In this down-on-its-luck town, isolation and a scarcity of goods and labor led to a culture of price-gouging and shoddy workmanship. Instead of trying to get ahead through hard work and initiative, most in the community tried to "milk" the summer people for everything they could get.

Jerome's parents felt that disloyalty to an employer was a form of theft, and they made sure that their kids were raised with a proper work ethic and a positive attitude. So, like so many other successful people, Jerome started working at an early age — mowing lawns and raking leaves.

A Lesson in Doing the Job Right

"A man with a vacation home needed some kids to rake leaves and clean the place up," he recalls. "The job was supposed to last about three days. Two of my friends and I went to rake leaves.

"My friends' parents had schooled them in the 'island attitude': Don't work too fast. Make this job stretch out because they're gonna pay you by the day. Stay as long as you can."

Jerome also got instructions from his father. "He told me to do my best and rake as fast as I could," he says. He remembers his Dad's words like this: "Don't be afraid of working yourself out of a job, because you'll always get another one. People recognize ambition and hard work."

So Jerome went to the other island where his friends were piling leaves at an almost leisurely pace. "I just started flying around," he remembers. "My friends got sent home. I finished the job, and the next-door neighbor hired me. I spent the whole season on that island, taking care of the houses and getting things fixed up. As a little kid I made an awful lot of money because I did the job ten times faster than anybody else."

I'm certain that "the summer people" didn't care how long it took Jerome to rake their leaves. They were delighted and impressed by a young man whose positive attitude and willingness to work hard made him stand out from the crowd, something that has continued throughout his life.

CHAPTER 40

Goals — The Seeds of Discipline

If you don't know where you are going, you might wind up someplace else.

— Yogi Berra

Let's assume that you have raised a wonderful child with self-discipline, a strong work ethic, and an ability to overcome adversity. There might still be something missing: the ability to set and achieve goals. Neglecting to teach a child how to set goals is like building a luxury cruise ship with swimming pools, ballrooms, cabins, and powerful diesel engines — and forgetting to install the helm, rudder, and compass.

A goal is sometimes defined as "a dream with a deadline." Children are dreamers. They dream about becoming musicians, athletes, and astronauts. Goal-setting separates the ones who achieve their dreams from the ones who look back at the might-have-beens.

Meet Barbara

In recent years, social scientists have produced volumes of work about the connection of goal attainment to personal happiness. Barbara Nolan knows this from personal experience. Her passion for goal-setting is a result of the positive changes that the practice has brought to her life.

"My dad gave me a great foundation," she says. "I didn't like it at the time. But he gave me a strong work ethic. He made me pay for everything. If I wanted to go to camp, I had to earn half. If I wanted a sweater that wasn't something I really needed to keep warm, I had to earn half. And he'd always go and inspect the lawn after I raked it. I always had to rerake or remow because he wanted it done just right.

"So, he taught me not to just do the job, but to do it well and to give more than was expected. It was hard work, and I hated it but it really did stand me in good stead in later years."

Written Goals Are a Source of Power

When Barbara started in sales, she approached my dad and asked what she could do to learn to excel. He gave her a copy of Earl Nightingale's audiotape *Lead the Field*, something he had listened to himself every morning for years.

Barbara calls that material "the missing piece." "I couldn't get enough of the principles that worked for all these successful people," she says. "The message was the same: set goals and make a plan for reaching them."

Barbara became a top salesperson, manager, and trainer, found the courage and grace to coparent two children, and the enthusiasm to give generously of her time to her many outside interests. "It's no secret," she says. "Goal-setting works for those who apply it."

CHAPTER 41

Go for the Goal

But what becomes of children's dreams? When adults say, "Don't be silly, or "You can't do that," who knows what kind of damage we are doing? Do we rob them of the opportunity to use their dreams to develop skills that will benefit them later in life?

Goal-setting is a learned skill. When you encourage children to pursue their dreams, you are helping them to develop a pattern of behavior that will guide their adult achievements. Here's an example that's close to my heart.

Ice Dreams

From about the second grade on, my son was determined to be a professional hockey player. He was obsessed. It was all he ever wanted to talk or think about. As far as he was concerned, he was in training to be a professional athlete. And while there were times that it drove me crazy, I didn't laugh at his dream. This is an excerpt from a school essay:

"It sometimes seems that I've dedicated my whole life to hockey. I spent ten years in Youth Hockey, skated Captains' practice at the college and banged a tennis ball into a net in the basement every day after school

til I was twelve. Through it all I played the way I was raised: work hard, follow your passion, and never complain to the coach.

Through the years these simple rules were never a problem — especially the first two. In the back of my mind I always wondered why the kids who whined were the ones getting the ice time. I never did understand why coaches rewarded such poor sportsmanship.

I failed to make the varsity team in my first year. For the next three years I worked harder than anyone did. In the weight room, tired and alone I asked myself why I was doing this, and I'd answer "for me."

My senior season flew by. I was a leader. I got to play a lot and it was the best season of my life. Even though I was a regular, I never stopped working, because I wanted to improve and I wanted the team to improve. We had a tough season with a lot of losses but the highlight of my hockey career came during the school's awards ceremony. I received the award for the most dedicated, hardworking leader. It is one of the most prestigious awards in the school's hockey program.

The most meaningful part of that award was I didn't have to do anything special to get it — just be the person I was raised to be. I think that is what I am most proud of. It shows that my mother raised me to be a good person."

Dreams are wonderful teachers. Growing up, I watched my dad set a goal and make a plan to reach it. I'm not sure how old I was when goal-setting became second nature for me.

I don't consider myself to be in the same class as the highest achievers, but I include this story to illustrate that one doesn't have to be in order to pass on these lessons. Having learned the Four Foundations, I was able to share them with my son. As a parent, you can begin to teach goal-setting at a young age both by example and helping your child set goals that relate to his interests.

CHAPTER 42

They Had Discipline and Goals

- Cal Ripken Jr. became baseball's new iron man, shattering Lou Gehrig's record by playing in 2,632 consecutive games for the Baltimore Orioles, taking the field despite sprains, strains, aches, and pains.
- Zen meditation masters are often able to exercise such discipline over their minds that they can sit in contemplation for days, and even control their own respiration and heart rates.
- According to a story on CNN *Money*, thirty-somethings Steven and Erica Ploof have saved and invested aggressively, to the point where they've turned a take-home income of about $4,000 a month into a mortgage that's 50% paid off and a retirement nest egg worth more than $340,000.
- Contortionists in the Cirque de Soleil begin training as young children and work for hours each day to develop the flexibility to bend their bodies into incredible positions.
- Ray Charles, blinded at the age of seven, ended up attending St. Augustine's, the Florida state school for the deaf and

blind, accepted as a charity student. There, he learned to read Braille and to type, and discovered mathematics and its connection to music. Through years of difficult repetition, he not only learned to read music by touch, but to compose and arrange scores in his head, separating the parts so that other musicians could play them. In time, he became a recording sensation and an American musical treasure commonly known as "The Genius."

- Union Grove, Wisconsin, high school student Bryan Guenzler finished his senior year without missing a single day of school — 13 years of perfect attendance since kindergarten. He says he "never gets sick enough to miss school."

- After spending years nearly fifty pounds overweight, Jenny Craig dropped the weight and kept it off, leading to the founding of her global weight loss empire.

- In 1651 at age forty three, John Milton lost his sight. However, his vision of an epic poem about man's fall from Eden led him to persevere as a writer, and he spent more than a decade working in darkness. In 1667, he published *Paradise Lost*.

- Offered the chance to complete two years of dental school in a single year, Steven Lawson and other students put in endless eighteen-hour days of study and clinical work with almost no breaks at a special dental program in San Francisco.

- *Apollo 13* astronauts Jim Lovell, Fred Haise, and Jack Swigert faced many kinds of death when their spacecraft lost most of its power and oxygen in an explosion on the way to the moon. But the discipline they had developed through years of repetitive training kept them alive and enabled them to return to earth safely.

CHAPTER 43

The Alpha Dog

You must do the thing you think you cannot do.

— Eleanor Roosevelt

The importance of establishing discipline and leadership is not unique to humans. The family dog and its ancestors offer valuable lessons about maintaining a safe and orderly family unit.

Puppies are pushy animals, always testing the limits and trying to advance as far as possible within their social structure. They become full-fledged pack members through a process called subordination, which begins when the pup is about three weeks old.

In a litter, the mother is the leader, responsible for the survival of the pack. Whether wolf or family pet, she nurtures, protects, and disciplines. She enforces the rules by grabbing the pup around the head or neck and, gently but firmly, pinning it on the ground.

"Alphas" are fair, firm and clear. They never nag. Sometimes their corrections are delivered with a look... other times with so much noise and drama that the issue never has to be revisited again. Pups quickly learn to greet adults with respect and behave within the guidelines of the pack.

Many parents are hesitant to enforce rules or take away privileges. They want to make all the hours they spend together at home happy and pleasant. But isn't it far easier to impose small disciplinary measures when our kids are young than to change bad habits later in life? Who else loves them enough to set the boundaries that will protect and guide them?

"One should guard against preaching to young people success in the customary form as the main aim in life. The most important motive for work in school and in life is pleasure in work, pleasure in its result, and the knowledge of the value of the result to the community."

— Albert Einstein

CHAPTER 44

Always on Duty

If there is anything we wish to change in the child, we should first examine it and see whether it is not something that could be better changed in ourselves.

— Carl Jung

How would you like to be followed by a video camera, with vivid color and complete sound recording capability, twenty four hours a day, seven days a week, every day for eighteen years? Guess what? If you're a parent, that's pretty much what's going on.

Don't believe me? Think about the last time you were around the parents of very small children who were spouting "bad" words? Why do they react with embarrassment?

Children learn through the examples of their role models, especially parents. Since in the formative years children mimic their parents, we must be attentive to our own habits and actions. Remember, in their early years kids learn rapidly, automatically and almost unconsciously. They are sponges, absorbing everything around them.

What Are They Learning from You?

One day my nephew accompanied Mark, a family friend, on a shopping trip. The clerk mistakenly rang up the sale as $38 instead of $380. They started to walk out of the store, joking about the error the clerk had made.

Suddenly, Mark recognized the example he was setting. They went back into the store and explained to the clerk what had happened. The clerk was grateful, the transaction was corrected, and Mark paid the correct amount.

How many of us would have spent an additional $342 just to set a good example? It would have been easy to rationalize the careless mistake. But Mark knew that honesty and integrity are not something to joke about. He wanted to make sure that his young friend had the advantage of seeing a trusted adult behave in a trustworthy manner — even when it would have been far easier to get away with doing something wrong.

Do you need to make any alterations for the benefit of your child's development and well-being?

"The success of humankind begins with the individual. If everyone understood the principles of personal achievement, who knows what humanity could achieve?"

— Mark Victor Hansen

CHAPTER 45

What Example

Are You Setting?

*You can get anything you want in this life if you help
other people get what they want.*

— Zig Ziglar

Paula McCarthy is the chief operating officer of a large marketing and management company. She is also another parent who paid close attention to the messages she sent to her children.

"When my son was in high school, he would go out with his friends after work in the summer," she says. "He always had a curfew. If he didn't come home at the agreed-upon time, I would get in the car and go looking for him. He learned that I meant business. My father was the same way with me. If I was supposed to be home and didn't call, he'd always pop up."

Lucky teens find out quickly that it is far less embarrassing to keep agreements with their parents than to have them show up unannounced. What you do has a far greater impact than what you say.

Hold Yourself to Your Own Standards

People who work with kids know how true this is. Not long ago, a policeman received a call from his headquarters about an illegally parked car outside the diner where he was getting coffee. When he looked out the diner window, he realized that his car was the one illegally parked. Instead of going out and moving his car, the officer wrote himself a ticket. He got his coffee, went to the courthouse, and paid for the parking violation.

Why did he go to the trouble? Part of his job was working with neighborhood kids who had probably made the call to the station. He knew that whether he held himself accountable or let himself off the hook the word of his example would travel fast and affect his work with the kids.

Like many single parents, Barbara Nolan worried about the impact that her career choices would have on her children. In retrospect, she feels that the example of discipline outweighed the occasional missed ballgame.

"I didn't have a nine-to-five job," she says. "I still did laundry, vacuumed the house, and yelled at them when they didn't make their beds. They had to contribute by doing chores, being responsible for their behavior, and staying out of trouble."

Barbara's sons are successful young men who have been able to apply the lessons of enthusiasm, optimism, and hard work to pursuing their own dreams and goals.

CHAPTER 46

Integrity on the Diamond

There are parents who don't understand that it is meaningless to say "I love you" to a child when her behavior doesn't back it up. Kids are smart. They know the difference between "talking the talk" and "walking the walk."

Ted Williams Takes a Pay Cut

If you want an example of integrity in action, you can't do much better than baseball legend Ted Williams. A star athlete and a hero in both World War II and the Korean War, he was a man who believed fiercely in doing what he believed was right.

Near the end of his career in 1959, a pinched nerve hampered his swing and his batting average dropped to just .254. It was the first time Williams had ever hit below .300 in his career, and he felt he had let his team, the Boston Red Sox, down. So he did something that in this era of spoiled, overpaid athletes would be unthinkable: he took a voluntary 30 percent pay cut.

The next year, Williams finished his career hitting .316. But more important was the integrity and honor he had shown the people of New England.

The Right Things for the Right Reasons

As Williams' example shows, it's more important to do the right thing than to take the easy path. That's what integrity is about: doing the right things for the right reasons. Children learn discipline from watching the choices their parents make. When we

"Success is not a destination that you ever reach. Success is the quality of your journey."

— Jennifer James

keep our word, when we follow through on a promise, we're sending a message: there's a right way to conduct oneself.

Integrity means being true to our values even when it's not convenient to do so. That's where the hard work, discipline, and persistence come in. When children live with the example of integrity, the Four Foundations make perfect sense.

Years ago, Sigmund Freud told us, "Love and work are the cornerstones of our humanness." Maybe he wasn't talking about two separate things. Maybe he was referring to the hard work and sacrifice that make love real. Like Ted Williams' love of the game.

CHAPTER 47

Teaching Financial Discipline

Lori Mackey counts herself luckier than her husband. "He had it a lot tougher than I did growing up," she says. "His parents said things like 'Money doesn't grow on trees.' I was much more fortunate. My parents taught me I could have anything I wanted if I was willing to pay the price — hard work."

By twenty one Lori was a successful hair stylist, teaching at salons across the country before starting her own exclusive salon. After more than twenty years in the beauty industry, she changed occupations and began to provide career training for a national conference firm. There she was exposed to some of the country's most prolific goal-setters and her next career was born.

The Entrepreneur for Kids

Money isn't evil; it's part of life. Children need to know that money is what makes the "things" they grow up with possible. Teaching them how to earn and manage it doesn't necessarily turn them into consumers. It makes them responsible.

Like it or not, money will play an important role in your child's life, including as a measure of her success and self-reliance. In the adult world, who will fare better: the child who is always given pocket money, or the one who had to earn it?

The Money Mama

Today Lori is known as "Money Mama." She's the founder of Prosperity4Kids, a company built on her vision that teaching kids about money is an important parental responsibility.

Lori's best-known product is an ingenious piggy bank that serves as a financial teaching tool for the preschool set. It's an old-fashioned porcelain piggy bank with a special twist: a large pig in the back (the 'money mama') with three little pigs in front — named Giving Pig, Savings Pig, and Investing Pig. When a child earns a dollar, parents help her divide it — with seventy cents going into money mama and a dime each into the others.

Lori's business has produced books, an online newsletter, allowance charts, and much more, all focused on teaching kids about earning, managing and investing money. But although Prosperity4Kids has been a financial success, she is much more passionate about the reasons why she started her business.

"It has allowed me to combine the things that I feel most passionately about: children, entrepreneurship, money, and teaching," Lori says. "Better still, we have been able to give thousands of dollars to children's charities while teaching children how to take control of their own financial lives and futures."

Lori understands that developing good financial habits early in life will go a long way to helping kids grow up to be self-reliant and appreciative of work. Financial discipline learned in the magic years can lead to healthy habits that will last a lifetime.

CHAPTER 48

On Discipline

Good habits result from resisting temptation. — Ancient Proverb

The happiness of a man in this life does not consist in the absence but in the mastery of his passions. — Alfred Lord Tennyson

Be still when you have nothing to say; when genuine passion moves you, say what you've got to say, and say it hot. — D. H. Lawrence

We improve ourselves by victories over ourself. There must be contests, and you must win. — Edward Gibbon

A mode of conduct, a standard of courage, discipline, fortitude and integrity can do a great deal to make a woman beautiful. — Jacqueline Bisset

Endurance is one of the most difficult disciplines, but it is to the one who endures that the final victory comes. — Buddha

Discipline is a symbol of caring to a child. He needs guidance. If there is love, there is no such thing as being too tough with a child.

— Bette Davis

Everybody starts at the top, and then has the problem of staying there. Lasting accomplishment, however, is still achieved through a long, slow climb and self-discipline.

— Helen Hayes

Genius at first is little more than a great capacity for receiving discipline.

— George Eliot

I think the years I have spent in prison have been the most formative and important in my life because of the discipline, the sensations, but chiefly the opportunity to think clearly, to try to understand things.

— Jawaharlal Nehru

Managers must have the discipline not to keep pulling up the flowers to see if their roots are healthy.

— Robert Townsend

No steam or gas ever drives anything until it is confined. No Niagara is ever turned into light and power until it is tunneled. No life ever grows until it is focused, dedicated, disciplined.

— Harry Emerson Fosdick

Persistence is self-discipline in action.

— Brian Tracy

Seek freedom and become captive of your desires. Seek discipline and find your liberty.

— Frank Herbert

PART FIVE

FOUNDATION #4

GIVING BACK

CHAPTER 49

Tying It All Together

When Dad started to write this book, he outlined it many times, but always felt something was missing. What was the other crucial childhood lesson that high-achieving adults had shared?

True Success Requires "Giving it Away"

Like so many parts of this story, the answer was almost too simple. While Dad recognized the generosity of those he had interviewed, it never really struck him that giving had played an important role in his own success. Like so many of the others we've interviewed, it's just part of who he is. Even his businesses are structured around helping people succeed.

Some who overcome adversity, develop a work ethic, and learn to be disciplined become self-centered. They can function, but leave a part of their potential untapped. As we said earlier, this is a book about giving your child a chance to be a superstar. I can't think of a single high achiever who really "went over the top" until he or she found a way to share his or her gifts with others.

Like the other three Foundations, giving does so much more good than is immediately apparent. It creates connection; it plugs us in to the rest of humanity. For many people it is the link that turns their faith to action, or the action that makes their values come alive. Teaching children how to give of their money, time, knowledge, effort, or compassion is a critical step in helping them make the transition from inward-turned individuals to outward-turned members of a community.

No One Succeeds Alone

Dad would be the first to tell you that without great mentors and colleagues, he wouldn't have achieved nearly as much as he has. But why did such talented individuals choose to work with him? In part, it's because, to the best of his ability, Dad gives of himself to others. After selling his company, he could have chosen to travel, play golf, or collect art. That lifestyle just didn't appeal to him. He went back to work, continuing to invest his time, talent, and effort, providing opportunity to those who follow.

Have you ever been to a fishing pier and seen the buckets of live crabs awaiting sale? While I doubt that they know that they're destined to become dinner, they don't like being confined. Crabs are rugged individuals, independent to a fault. When one tries climb out of the barrel, the others seem to pull it back down. Imagine if they'd learned to act selflessly — eventually they could all reach the top and everyone would be free. It's exactly the same for people. No one reaches their full potential unless giving to others is a natural part of how they live.

Giving Inspires Others to Give

Success is built on relationships. Whether your goal is to build a business, play on a team, or create a family, it doesn't work without other people. Even a solitary artist needs others; without a patron to show his work or an audience to enjoy it, the cycle of creativity remains incomplete. No high achiever reaches a position of wealth, fulfillment, advanced education, or acclaim without many people lending a hand along the way.

Contrary to popular opinion, the road to success is lined with relationships. They are replete with loyalty, kindness and mentoring. Opportunities are created by people committed to serving others — behaving in a manner that shows that they care about more than themselves. Real success is never built solely on self-interest.

Now wait a minute, you might say. Don't people often give with the hope of getting something back? Sometimes. But what if the person to whom they are giving has nothing to give back? What compels a person to open doors for someone who appears to have nothing to give back? What about mentoring?

I have been mentored in a number of disciplines. Although rarely spelled out, the rules were always the same: uphold a higher standard than my peers by working harder and producing better results, often for less money.

What did my mentors get? Someone who admired and respected them enough to want to learn everything they knew. And I'm sure some of them recognized their "younger selves," eager to work, learn, and excel. When I had the chance to be a mentor, I learned firsthand just how fulfilling it could be.

Maybe people don't give to get. Maybe they get more and become more so they have more to give.

Dad and his businesses are full of examples of how this works. Up and down the line, there are partnerships and teams: one person provides experience, training, guidance, and financing while another brings hard work and burning desire. And everyone who gets an opportunity is expected to pass it on.

Sales managers assign "buddies" to the newest hires; more experienced office managers pass on time- and moneysaving tips to the newer ones; promotions that work in one part of the country are tried in others. There's competition but never at the expense of what is good for the whole organization. When someone does well, everyone gets a chance to improve.

Giving Back is the Bridge to the World

Those who give of their energy, ideas and time — without worrying about what it's going to get them — inspire others to do more. No matter how tired and cynical an executive has become, she's still likely to be warmed by the sparks thrown off by a young up-and-comer with a true passion for the job.

Are you raising a child who will live her ideals and inspire others? A work ethic, discipline, and the ability to overcome obstacles puts kids in a position to become successful adults. The ability to give to others strengthens the relationships that bring that success to light. By teaching children about giving, we help make it a natural part of their lives.

CHAPTER 50

Giving Becomes
Inevitable

People sometimes deprive themselves of all the good that comes from giving because they don't have a lot of money. Please don't make that mistake.

What kind of giving are we talking about? Not just giving money to charitable or religious organizations, although that's certainly important. Everyone can give their time, their effort, their attention, or their ideas to make a difference. We all have these things in abundance. When giving is part of the fabric of their lives, children can become adults who regularly contribute to the betterment of their communities. When a child has internalized the first three Foundations, giving becomes the next logical step.

Giving to others is a natural by-product of being raised on the other Foundations. So in a sense, if you're raising a child whose character has been shaped by discipline, hard work, and meeting every challenge, you're already raising someone who will be inclined to give to others. You just need to show them how.

Strength of Character Leads to Giving

A child who works hard, is disciplined, and gets back up after a fall is more likely to share her money, time, and knowledge with others.

Why? For one thing, she's going to be extremely self-confident: she has something important to share with the world. For another, her life of work has given her a deep appreciation for what she has, so she's more apt to help those with less. Her work history has also taught her that all kinds of work are important, making her more likely to support the work and commitment of others by volunteering her money or time. And she's probably had a mentor or two, so she's likely to be one herself, repaying that gift by paying it forward.

Giving Is Just What Successful People Do

If you're not convinced, do your own research. Talk to the most successful people in your community. A warning: when you ask them about their donations or fund-raising, there's probably not going to be much conversation. Many people have been taught to give in secret and are uncomfortable with recognition. It diminishes the pleasure associated with giving.

Instead, you might talk to the people around the givers. I'll bet you find that the vast majority of the high achievers in your community give time, talent, and treasure to a private foundation, a local hospital or performing arts center, or contribute to the welfare of others in some way. If you ask them why they do it, you'll probably hear something like, "It's just important to me," or, "I've been very fortunate," or, "Someone did the same for me."

CHAPTER 51

Other Benefits
of Giving

*Small opportunities are often the
beginning of great enterprises.*

— Demosthenes

Children are born selfish. Biology insists that newborns focus only on their own needs: food, a clean diaper, being held, and so on. That's natural. It's a survival instinct. As they become bigger and stronger, it's our job as parents to *teach* them about others' needs.

When kids see us delivering meals to the homebound or taking unused clothing to the Salvation Army, it is as natural for them to want to come along as it is for them to ask "Why?"

This is the point in a child's life where we can begin to help him understand that part of the price for living in this world is helping others. That giving back is a joy and a privilege. Teaching generosity early in life helps to develop a giving reflex that is as natural as breathing.

You *Do* Get More than You Give

My dad is far more comfortable being generous than talking about it. When I asked him how he learned to give, he told me that it was something he heard when he was very young. "I heard that whatever you give comes back tenfold," he said. "I did and it did."

When you give to others, you get back more. More opportunity, better relationships, goodwill, help when you need it, and so on. All religious and spiritual traditions tell us this is true. Eastern religions call it karma, popular culture tells us "what goes around comes around," and Christianity tells us "as ye sow, so shall ye reap." Twelve Step programs get in on the act, telling us "to keep what we have we must give it away."

Easier to Understand

That's a wonderful concept. But children may need more immediate rewards for what they do. Here are a few benefits that are even easier to see and understand:

- Kids who volunteer connect with other people who share their passions or concerns.
- Getting involved puts them in a position to be liked and appreciated by adults who aren't their parents.
- Colleges and universities look at service as part of the admissions process; many scholarships are given for such service.
- Sharing what we have with those in need opens our eyes, and can help us to appreciate what we have. Our grandparents called this "counting our blessings."

CHAPTER 52

Compassion

Is a Choice

When Rick was a kid, what he wanted life to be safe, fair, and predictable. His first job, at about age nine, was going to the bank to make the mortgage payment. His heart would pound the entire distance from his mother's doorstep to the relative safety of the bank lobby. After all, even in sleepy New England towns, there are people who are willing to take things that aren't theirs. And as the man of the house, Rick just couldn't let that happen.

But even the racing heart and sweaty palms he experienced while protecting the mortgage money were nothing compared with what he had felt back when he wasn't the man of the house — when his father made life a daily ordeal.

After years of failing and abusing his family, Rick's father finally left town one day. But Rick's character had already been shaped by his early experiences. And with violence and struggle in the background, I was a bit surprised to discover that this duty-driven man feels that it was the absence of a father that most influenced his character and outlook on life.

Channeling Adversity into Service

So what does a young man do when he has been abandoned by the person who is supposed to teach him how to be a man? How does he harness a blend of deep empathy, independence, insatiable curiosity, and a desire to be a different kind of a man from his father?

In Rick Gauthier's case, he put himself through school and became a cop. Not only does law enforcement appeal to his sense of fairness and his protective nature, but his innate mistrust of others' motives makes him an excellent investigator.

His work ethic resulted in excellent attendance, continued training and "extra" reading. He took the assignments no one else wanted and learned to excel when dealing with child abuse and domestic violence...areas in which he already knew too much.

Rick worked his way up the chain of command, eventually becoming the chief of police in his hometown. He also attained the stable, comfortable family life he had always wanted. You might think a career in public service would be enough. Not as far as Rick's concerned. If you're getting paid for it, it's not giving. So he commits both his free time and finances to a variety of important civic causes, ranging from mentoring to twenty years of volunteer service with the community agency that serves victims of domestic violence and sexual assault.

Dignity and Grace

I know Rick and admire him for his integrity and complete dedication to giving his best to others. But there are many stories that illustrate that point better than I ever could.

Sally was chronically mentally ill, a mother of nine who had managed to break enough rules to wear out her welcome with the local health and public safety community. In a last ditch effort to stabilize her family life and keep her children out of foster care, the family court judge had ordered her to work with my program. Despite the team's best efforts, things were not looking good.

One day I went to Sally's house, and she informed me that she had been assaulted. So I called Rick, who was then working as a detective. "It doesn't matter what her history is," he said. "It's our responsibility to try to get the facts in case something really *did* happen." He met us at the hospital and took her statement with complete professionalism, compassion, and sensitivity.

Time and again I watched him take the high road. Once a suspect used a church meditation group to hide out and avoid arrest. Acting on a tip from a member of the group, Rick arranged to wait outside for this violent felon and quietly made the arrest without entering the church or disrupting worship.

Other incidents involve a decision he would rarely condone in his officers, primarily for the obvious safety concerns. When removing a suspect from a home where children live, Rick often negotiates a level of cooperation that allows him to escort a suspect out of a building without the use of handcuffs... sparing kids a scarring and humiliating sight.

What You Give Comes Back

Rick's occupation has offered him many opportunities to meet callousness with callousness, cruelty with cruelty. But he chose to rise above how others treated him, and in doing so, made himself a finer human being, admired by many. One could argue that how he chose to respond to the events of his life — with compassion and generosity — have led to the life he enjoys today. Whether in spite or because of the lessons of his early years, Rick has remembered the most important rule: what you give comes back to you.

TEN RULES OF GIVING

Children should be offered guidelines for giving. Here are some to consider:

1. Giving is done without any thought of reward, recognition, or compensation.

2. Giving is consistent, so you're helping not once but again and again.

3. Give to what you care about.

4. When you make a commitment to give, always keep it. People are depending on you.

5. Give what you can, and no more. Every little bit makes a difference.

6. Caring for others is good for you, like eating your vegetables. Sometimes you have to do it even if you don't feel like it. And it's still good for you.

7. When people thank you for giving, thank them for opportunity to serve.

8. Always do the best job you can and work as hard as you can.

9. Never look down on others who "don't give". You have no idea of their reasons. Besides, they may be giving to someone else — anonymously.

10. Enjoy the feeling of making someone else's life better. It's wonderful.

53

Giving Feels Good

Yesterday I dared to struggle. Today I dare to win.

— Bernadette Devlin

Welcome to the cynical portion of our program. At least, that's how it sounds when I propose that giving is truly a selfish act. But it's not cynicism; it's simple truth, and recognizing the selfish nature of giving can be a wonderful tool for parents trying to motivate their children to be generous with their time and their treasure.

Why do we give? Of course, we want to help people in need or help advance a cause that's important to us. But people give for lots of different reasons:

- They believe in a mission
- Someone close to them has benefited from an organization
- They want to improve the community in which they live
- To honor or memorialize someone

- To feel appreciated
- They know and respect someone who is already involved

Giving has its altruistic motives. Many of the largest gifts are given anonymously. But why not be purely selfish and focus only on our own well-being?

That's the point. When we give, that's what we're doing. We're taking care of ourselves by taking care of others. Paying it forward. Making a deposit in the First National Bank of Karma. Doing unto others as we would have done to us.

When the wealthy donate money for a university building or a community theater, they are being philanthropic. They may also be creating a legacy. No one condemns them for it.

Giving Is a Natural High

Giving feels good. Is there anything wrong with this? I don't think so. It's natural to want to feel good about ourselves, and to want the approval of others. Few things make people feel better than giving to others. That's why giving to charities or volunteering for nonprofits often leads to doing more; in a society that's often focused on material gain, it puts us in touch with our values and makes us feel better.

As your children become aware of the importance of giving, it's probably not a bad idea to make them aware of the "selfish" feelings they will get from the act of giving, and that these feelings are okay. More than okay, they are, in fact, one of the ways that giving really does give more to the giver.

CHAPTER 54

Mentoring — a Gift
That Gives to Everyone

When Tony Cersosimo decided to invest in my father's business, Dad got more than a business partner. Tony was older and more experienced. Dad says, "I liked being around him; I usually learned something." He was a mentor.

The concept of mentoring dates back to ancient Greece. The word usually describes a relationship of trust and passing on of wisdom between two people of different generations. Good mentors offer support, challenge, patience, and enthusiasm while guiding others to new levels of achievement.

A Surrogate Father

Tony picked up Dad's education where Grampa Pat left off. Their relationship lasted more than thirty years and was an important source of support, guidance, and inspiration for my dad. Tony set a fine example in every area of his life.

"From the beginning, I respected both his values and his accomplishments," Dad says. "Tony was a tough taskmaster but rarely missed an opportunity to give a helping hand to someone less experienced or less fortunate than himself."

Tony's word was his bond. Together they created a partnership worth millions of dollars, but there was never a written document. "He taught me that if a man was good enough to be your partner, his word was better than all the paper an army of attorneys could generate," Dad says.

Giving Back the Gift

You'll rarely find a high achiever who hasn't either had a mentor, been one, or both. The reason behind this is simple: nothing teaches like experience, and no matter how bright and educated our kids are, they lack life experience. Mentoring is about passing on life lessons to others, sharing the mistakes made and the reasons behind the victories, in order to help a younger person learn and avoid old missteps. Or as one wise man put it, "to make all new mistakes."

Mentoring Programs

Any child can benefit from a mentor. Great mentors teach more than specific skills. They expose kids to new areas of endeavor, new ways of thinking, new adults who teach by example as much as by words. They can be teachers, bosses at early jobs, friends of the family, grandfathers — anyone with the patience and desire to pass on wisdom and "walk the walk" can be a mentor.

There's one more good reason to introduce children to the concept of mentoring, aside from the life lessons it can impart to them: there's no better way to pass on the love of mentoring than to have a wonderful mentor yourself. Most successful people take pride and joy in mentoring others the same way they were mentored. In this way, we pass life's best lessons down through the generations.

CHAPTER 55

How Strong Is Their "Why?"

My friend Mark Victor Hansen is a successful person who has embraced his opportunities to give. He's the co-creator of one of the world's most successful book series, a best-selling author, and motivational speaker who's in demand around the world. Yet Mark makes time every year to raise funds for the fight against hunger or some other worthy cause, and he gives his time and money to causes about which he cares deeply. Literacy is one of them, and when he talks about literacy and his Danish parents, the emotional crack in his voice is 100% real. This is a man for whom giving is very personal.

But Mark doesn't "need" to give back to fit the conventional idea of success. He's a wealthy, successful man for whom time is tight. Every day is a full-tilt whirlwind of business demands, travel, speaking, marketing, and more. He could think only of himself and still be wildly successful in monetary terms. So how does Mark find the time and means to give so much of himself to these causes? "If you have the 'why,' the 'how' takes care of itself," he says.

Giving Should Always Be Personal

That means that if your child finds a cause that fires his passion for giving, he'll find a way to make it happen. Busy, successful people don't worry about how they'll balance their schedules with the causes they believe in; they just do it.

That's why you see celebrities like Art Linkletter traveling the country to raise money to find a cure for Alzheimer's Disease, or professional athletes reading books to children in schools. They care deeply and personally about giving to the causes that mean the most to them.

Encourage Discovery of the World of Need

In raising children for whom giving back is an instinct and a delight, it's important to give them free rein to discover the areas of giving that matter to them. These may not be the same as yours; that's fine. But while it's important to teach children about the benefits and reasons behind generosity, it's just as important to stand back and let them discover what they care about.

Curious children with a desire to make a difference in their world are the ones who join the Peace Corps after college, who go on "volunteer vacations" to help fund and participate in scientific research, who start neighborhood coalitions and try to better their communities. By teaching the fundamentals of giving (the "how") and then standing back and letting kids discover their personal "why," we encourage them to develop the passion, empathy, and determination that will make them the adults that we can truly admire.

CHAPTER 56

A Life of Purpose

Every great achievement is the victory
of a flaming heart.

— Ralph Waldo Emerson

Take the question of "why" to its full extent, and you have purpose. Most of us have many purposes in our lives. We want to "raise a happy family," "be a good person," "serve our community," and so on. Commendable ideas, every one.

But then there are those people whose lives revolve around a single reason, a single mission, whether it's to eradicate AIDS or feed the hungry. They're single-minded individuals who we might not want to emulate, but we can't help but respect. They are people with purpose.

Giving defines purpose. It's that simple. You rarely find someone who proudly tells you that their purpose in life is to own the latest Porsche or to grow the best lawn in the county. Purpose always stems from giving. It's "why" to the nth degree, and those with a sense of purpose usually bring great passion, dedication, and energy not just to their mission, but to life.

The Saint of Calcutta

Few lives in the modern age reflect the power of a life of purpose like the life of Mother Teresa. The tiny Albanian nun, whose face and name became famous the world over, was born as Agnes Gonxha Bojaxhiu in 1910 in a town in what was then Yugoslavia.

"One should guard against preaching to young people success in the customary form as the main aim in life. The most important motive for work in school and in life is pleasure in work, pleasure in its result, and the knowledge of the value of the result to the community."

— Albert Einstein

From an early age, she wanted to work in India. As a young girl, she went to Ireland to become a nun. Although she knew God had called her, it was still hard to leave home. But once she took action, she never doubted that she was on the right path.

Sister Teresa became principal of her school, but at age thirty six, she had her "inspiration day." An "inner voice" told her to give up everything and serve the poorest of the poor — the hungry, the sick, and the dying people of Calcutta. She believed this to be God's call.

A Tireless Advocate for the Poor

She moved to Calcutta and began ministering to the poor, orphans, the sick and the dying. In 1950, she formed a new religious order, the Missionary Sisters of Charity. The work was backbreaking, but her purpose drove her. When she wasn't caring for these desperately needy people, she traveled to speak to groups like the United Nations, asking powerful nations to help the world's most powerless. Mother Teresa was widely hailed as a living "saint of the gutters," and, in 1979, received the Nobel Peace Prize.

This is a woman who, by any definition, was a success. She moved people to service and raised millions of dollars to support her work. The Missionary Sisters of Charity can now be found all over the world. When she died in 1997 she owned three items: two saris (simple Indian-style clothing) and a bucket in which to wash them.

"Success is to be measured not so much by the position that one has reached in life as by the obstacles which he has overcome while trying to succeed."

— Booker T. Washington

Support Passion and Discovery

A child with a sense of purpose won't necessarily end up devoting his life to a single cause to the exclusion of all else. Not all purpose-filled individuals end up living their lives in the extreme. Most live regular lives with families and friends. But much of the

"You can have unbelievable intelligence, you can have connections, you can have opportunities fall out of the sky. But in the end, hard work is the true, enduring characteristic of successful people."

— Marsha Evans

energy that others put into shopping or camping, they put into sorting donated clothing, teaching boating safety, or rescuing abandoned pets.

Should you encourage purpose in your child? It's really not something any of us can control. Your child may never discover a single purpose. But we can encourage kids to explore and discover, to be passionate about causes and people in need, and to take action when it is needed. In this way, we can make the ground fertile for any seeds our children choose to plant.

CHAPTER 57

Service Requires Excellence

Success is not the key to happiness. Happiness is the key to success. If you love what you are doing, you will be successful.

— Albert Schweitzer

High achievers serve others. Being able to give back implies that you are successful enough — have moved far enough beyond survival mode — that you can afford to give of your time or money for the benefit of strangers. And if a person is looking for an opportunity to pass on knowledge, he or she had better be reasonably successful at his or her chosen field. Not many schools, parents, or companies are looking for failures as mentors. The irony is, through giving we become successful.

But there's more to it than that. Giving to others often brings the "rising tide lifts all boats" concept into play. If one person does well, all do well. You see this dynamic at work on Little

League teams where one player lays down a sacrifice bunt so another can score.

Serving others strengthens responsibility, which is why the other three Foundations all tie in to it. When your child commits to give time or effort to others, he's promising to perform. He's making the church or charity group dependent on his ability to deliver what he says he'll deliver, whether it's money through fund-raising or volunteers for a recycling program. When you serve, you've got to excel. There's really no other choice.

Giving Brings Out the Best

On the flip side of this whole issue, serving others also inspires kids and adults to do more than they may have thought possible. When we serve, we often feel that we're connected to a higher purpose. Giving uplifts the giver as much as it does those around him.

Those who habitually give demand more of themselves and others, use their time more productively, and tend to be more successful in all endeavors. Giving teaches and demands excellence; that's one of its greatest rewards.

"Achievement seems to be connected with action. Successful men and women keep moving. They make mistakes, but they don't quit."

— Conrad Hilton

CHAPTER 58

They Gave Because
They *Had* To

- Hundreds of firefighters at the World Trade Center on September 11 rushed into the burning buildings knowing they were probably signing their own death warrants, but it was their job to try to save others who were trapped.
- Ladder 10, the company of firefighters that lost so many in the terrorist attack, tells of homeless people in the area bringing the firemen their cups of coins, while a crippled woman from the Bronx came down to donate her cane to survivors, and a Georgia boy mailed his penny bank to volunteers.
- John Walsh suffered the agony of losing his son, Adam, to a murderer who was never convicted of the crime. But he turned his pain into a life as a tireless advocate for victim's rights and missing children, and into *America's Most Wanted*, a TV show that has contributed to the capture of more than eight hundred fugitives.
- Pat Tillman turned his back on a multi-million-dollar National Football League contract to join the army, become

a Ranger, and serve in Iraq and Afghanistan, where he was killed in 2004.

- Bill and Melinda Gates, the richest couple in the world thanks to the success of Microsoft, also run the world's largest private foundation. Through it they donate hundreds of millions of dollars to improve health care around the world, including fighting the spread of AIDS.

- In 1982, Oscar-winning actor Paul Newman and a friend turned their home salad dressing hobby into a specialty food business, Newman's Own, and decided to donate all the profits from the business to charity. To date, they have donated more than $150 million to various organizations.

- Jackie Robinson knew he would open himself to a torrent of racist abuse, hatred, and violence by stepping onto the diamond as the first African-American baseball player. But he did it anyway, saying that it was important for his race.

- A self-made millionaire with a suffering family life, Millard Fuller changed the course of his life at twenty nine to found Habitat for Humanity and dedicate his life to building homes for needy families worldwide.

- Millions of people, many of whom have never been personally touched by the diseases, participate in charity walks, runs and bicycle races to raise money for diseases such as ALS and breast cancer.

- Thousands of healthy people risk their lives every year donating kidneys, lungs and other organs to loved ones (and sometimes to perfect strangers).

CHAPTER 59

Giving Is an Art

Michael Johnson has Down Syndrome. He's also a successful artist. His colorful, impressionistic paintings of animals are extremely popular. His work has appeared on T-shirts, posters, and magazine covers. But I didn't know the man behind the paintings had such a huge heart until I ordered some of his work.

Like many children, Michael enjoyed drawing with markers and crayons. When he graduated from Park School in Evanston, Illinois, he received some art supplies. They so captured his imagination that he was asked, "Do you want to be an artist?" His firm reply? "I *am* an artist."

Discipline, Hard Work and Self-Reliance

Michael discovered that he had not only a talent for painting, but a gift for animal portraiture, as well. In a few short years, what began as a hobby has become a thriving mail-order business. But that's not what's so impressive about Michael. In a way, he embodies all the Four Foundations.

Early in his life, he and his mother had to cope with his Down Syndrome while living with an abusive man. After they were able to escape, Michael's discipline came from a loving mother who found a school that supported her core belief: Michael would be capable of doing in the future whatever he was allowed to do for himself today.

She wanted him to get support and instruction, of course, but also to learn the skills that he needed to take care of himself. So that's how Michael's school experience went: he did as much as he could for himself. His work ethic began there.

A Talent for Charity

But that's still not what really impressed me about Michael. I ordered several of his smaller paintings off his Web site — some for myself and some as gifts. When the package arrived, I was pleasantly surprised at both the quality and the quantity of what was in the package.

I recognized the paintings I had ordered, and they were even nicer than what I had seen in the catalog. But there was something else in the box. A painting that I hadn't ordered. As I started to think about returning it, I discovered the note that came with it: "When people buy three or more, I always include an extra….I hope that you find a way to use it as a fund-raiser for the animal rescue group of your choice. Your friend, Michael."

I was surprised and humbled. Here was a young man who most would consider disabled, in need of the compassion of others, and he was going out of his way to help homeless animals. It wasn't a tool to sell more paintings or get press coverage. It was Michael's way of doing good. He has a generosity of spirit that's at least as remarkable as his art.

CHAPTER 60

On Giving

You must give some time to your fellow men. Even if it's a little thing, do something for others — something for which you get no pay but the privilege of doing it."　　　— Albert Schweitzer

The great art of giving consists in this: the gift should cost very little and yet be greatly coveted, so that it may be the more highly appreciated.　　　— Baltasar Gracian

Make all you can, save all you can, give all you can.
　　　— John Wesley

You try to give away what you want yourself.
　　　— Lois McMaster Bujold

Generosity during life is a very different thing from generosity in the hour of death; one proceeds from genuine liberality and benevolence, the other from pride or fear.　　　— Horace Mann

Purchase not friends by gifts; when thou ceasest to give, such will cease to love. — Thomas Fuller

For anything worth having one must pay the price; and the price is always work, patience, love, self-sacrifice—no paper currency, no promises to pay, but the gold of real service. — John Burroughs

Self-sacrifice is the real miracle out of which all the reported miracles grow. — Ralph Waldo Emerson

It is every man's obligation to put back into the world at least the equivalent of what he takes out of it. — Albert Einstein

No one has ever become poor by giving. — Anne Frank

There is a wonderful mythical law of nature that the three things we crave most in life — happiness, freedom, and peace of mind — are always attained by giving them to someone else. — Payton Conway March

Real generosity toward the future lies in giving all to the present. — Albert Camus

I have found that among its other benefits, giving liberates the soul of the giver. — Maya Angelou

CHAPTER 61

Some Final Thoughts

Chance favors the prepared mind.

— Louis Pasteur

This may strike you a little funny at first, but here goes. I'm going to miss you.

That's right. You. Although we've never met, I've been thinking about you every day for a long time. About your worries and your struggles, your hopes and dreams. The guilt so many like you feel when things just aren't smooth.

We've shared some interesting moments, as well. Like trying to get out the door with a child who hates the only pair of shoes you've been able to find. Listening to the tears that followed the grade when you held your ground and didn't actually *do* the sixth grade science project for your child. Even the time you spent too much on the latest greatest electronic doodad that your kid *had* to have, and beat yourself up over it for three days. I've been remembering what that all feels like.

I've been imagining some of your questions, too. "Do they really think it's that easy?" "Is this everything I need to know?" What if I didn't grow up with this stuff? Does that mean I can't teach it to my kids?" "My kid is ten. Is it too late?" "What *about* love?"

You Already Know the Answers

Relax. You know the answers. It's not easy, yes you can do it, and there's always a lot to learn. Reading uplifting stories about people who have succeeded with the Four Foundations does not mean you can't also learn about developmental milestones or differences in personalities and learning styles. Quite the contrary. There are lots of great books and classes on those topics. I encourage you to take advantage of them.

What about love? Even in the darkest of circumstances I would be hard-pressed to think of a parent whose choices were motivated by anything else. Parents love. Because of that they want to do more and better. Figuring out what that looks and feels like can be a daunting task.

Guilt, Thy Name Is Spelled *D-A-D* or *M-O-M*

There is so much conflicting advice about the best way to raise kids that it's hard to know what to do. We help with homework, expose them to the arts, make sure they get exercise, and answer all of the "why is the sky blue?" questions while cleaning the house and bringing home a paycheck. Sound familiar? It's no wonder we feel like we've run a marathon every day of the week.

Like any other part of life, raising a child is full of choices and compromise. No one can do everything. But what are the right things to give up or postpone? After meeting basic needs, the answer really depends upon what you want to achieve. What are your priorities for your child's future?

Every time we choose in favor of something, we choose against something else. But no matter what we choose, it's not difficult to find someone to help us feel guilty. Too strict. Too permissive. Nurturing. Stifling. Indulgent. Quality time with kids..... living vicariously through them.....and on and on and on.

What Is a Good Parent?

The definition of good parenting might depend on whom you ask! Two- and three-year-olds give gold stars to parents who let them watch lots of cartoons, eat chocolate chip cookies for breakfast, and stay up as late as they want. Eight- and nine-year-olds give thumbs-up to parents who do their homework for them, let the chores slide, and intervene with the coach and the teacher. Thirteen- to fifteen-year-olds approve of parents who provide credit cards, cell phones, late curfews, and smoking or drinking.

Clearly, cookies and parties aren't the issue. Too many parents are afraid to say no to their kids, fearing that any discomfort is going to cause irreparable harm. Parents who set standards and limits are often considered ogres, ridiculed and shunned by the permissive crowd. Too many back down. It's like being back in high school — giving in to peer pressure so everybody can feel good about themselves right now. Aren't we supposed to have outgrown that behavior?

A New Lens

Most people don't set out in search of obstacles to overcome. Most of us don't need to. Obstacles just show up — usually when they're least expected and most inconvenient. But what if, instead

"I've never sought success in order to get fame and money: it's the talent and the passion that count."

— Ingrid Bergman

of seeing them as barriers, you could see them as inevitable, necessary, and full of gifts?

I hope that's what Dad and I have given you: a new lens through which to view the inevitable ups and downs that go with being a parent. So much depends on training and attitude. Challenges arise whether we believe we're ready to learn or not. Maybe remembering that everyone has tough times will help you to stay true to your plan and consistent in the face of criticism. The Chinese symbol for "crisis" is made of the symbols for "danger" and "opportunity." Which part of the symbol is going to attract your attention and energy? You already know what we think. We wish you the best as you decide for yourself.

So how do we say good-bye for now? In the same way we've said everything else: with one last story.

Distinguished Americans

If there's a single group that illustrates the impact of the Four Foundations, it's the Horatio Alger Association of Distinguished Americans. Founded in 1947, this organization has a simple but inspiring mission: to honor the achievements of Americans who have succeeded after overcoming great hardships. The Association honors the hard work and discipline that has taken its members from humble beginnings to peak performance in every arena. And they do this, in large part, by reaching out to struggling young people to provide support in the form of mentoring combined with millions of dollars in college scholarship money.

The membership list of the Horatio Alger Association reads like a *Who's Who of American Achievement*. It's also a tribute to the power of hard work, persistence, discipline and generosity. Today's Horatio Alger Heroes invariably cite the lessons of their youth as critical to success as they understand and experience it today.

Rags to Riches Tales

The real Horatio Alger Jr. was a writer born in Revere, Massachusetts, in 1832. During his decades-long career, he wrote more than 120 novels. They shared a basic plot line: a young boy with few prospects but an abundance of integrity, perseverance, kindness, and enthusiasm would work his way to the top. Alger's novels delivered a message of hope to Americans of his era: if you're honest, hard working, self-reliant and try to do the right thing, you will succeed.

A Galaxy of Achievers

Today, the Association has nearly six hundred distinguished members. You've already met one of them, Brigadier General Sherian Grace Cadoria. And true to the general's example, the membership list is an astonishing roll call of brilliance, courage, leadership and chutzpah. Other examples include media mogul Oprah Winfrey, the late singer-songwriter Johnny Cash, Mark Victor Hansen, pediatric neurosurgeon Dr. Ben Carson, business moguls Conrad Hilton, H. Ross Perot and Wally "Famous" Amos, and the first international member, hockey legend Wayne Gretzky. They're but a few of the people in this organization who have triumphed over adversity and achieved victory when others quit. Now they help others make the same journey. In a very real way, the members of the Horatio Alger Association represent the best of us. Not because of their wealth or notoriety, but because they embody so many time-tested American values. When you sit in a room with the living members gathered together, as both my father and I have been privileged to do, it's overwhelming, humbling, and inspiring.

The Foundations Brought to Life

So why did we choose to close this book with the Association? Because it is an impressive collection of successful people whose lives were shaped by the Four Foundations. They're from many backgrounds, races and professions. As one of their leaders recently said, they represent "a democracy of opportunity and an aristocracy of achievement."

They learned to work hard, probably because most came from poor backgrounds and work was a matter of survival. Many became wealthy; some are not. They learned to get back up after a failure, because failure happens to everyone and something — or some*one* — didn't let them quit. They learned to follow rules, meet expectations, and act according to a certain standard of behavior set down by their parents, their church or their community. And they discovered the joy of giving. That's one thing you learn quickly when you start meeting Horatio Alger Association members: their generosity of spirit is incredible.

A Resource for Children

Are we suggesting you raise your child with an eye on getting him or her a Horatio Alger Award? Of course not. The prize for raising a successful adult is fulfillment, purpose, and a sense of giving and receiving from others. We offer the association as a sort of compass, proof of what can be accomplished — and to make some of you aware that this resource may be available to give your child a helping hand.

On the practical side, the organization recognizes outstanding students in many ways: with scholarships and financial aid, and with its National Scholars Conference, in which selected students gather in Washington, D.C., to spend time with leaders from business, the arts and government. Such recognition and support can propel a child to a lifetime of success.

Good Human Beings

But beyond all that — the awards, the recognition, the achievements — what we're trying to do is give you one more way to show children how to reach their full potential. That's what you'll find at the Horatio Alger Association: examples of humans at their finest. Their field of endeavor doesn't matter. What matters is that throughout their lives, they have conducted themselves with honor, intelligence, kindness, vision, humor, and a sense of duty to others.

Is there a better way to end than with this example of what our children could grow up to become?

Now the task falls to you. Are you ready?

Harry S. Patten
Andrea Patten
Williamstown, Massachusetts
October 2004

INTERESTING READING

Andrews, Robert. *The Concise Columbia Dictionary of Quotations.* Avon Books, New York. 1987.

Blanchard, Ken and Cathy, S. Truett. *The Generosity Factor.* Zondervan Publishing, Grand Rapids, MI. 2002.

Bledsoe, Mac. *Parenting with Dignity.* Alpha Books, Indianapolis, IN. 2003.

Canfield, Jack and Hansen, Mark Victor, et al. *Chicken Soup for the Mother's Soul.* Health Communications, Inc. Deerfield, FL. 1997.

Canfield, Jack and Hansen, Mark Victor. *A Third Serving of Chicken Soup for the Soul.* Health Communications, Inc. Deerfield, FL. 1996.

Canfield, Jack, Hansen, Mark Victor and Hewitt, Les. *The Power of Focus.* Health Communications, Inc. Deerfield, FL. 2000.

Carmichael, Bill and Nancie. *The Best Things Ever Said About Parenting.* Tyndale House Publishers, Wheaton, IL. 1996.

Clark, Ron. *The Essential 55.* Hyperion, New York. 2003.

Cline, Foster W., M.D. and Fay, Jim. *Parenting with Love and Logic.* Pinion Press, Colorado Springs, CO. 1992.

Csikszentmihalyi, Mihaly. *Flow.* Harper Collins, New York. 1990.

Davidson, Alan, PhD & Davidson, Robert. *How Good Parents Raise Great Kids.* Warner Books, New York. 1996.

Davis, Wynn. *The Best of Success.* Great Quotations Publishing Company, Lombard, IL. 1988.

DeGraff, John, Wann, David and Naylor, Thomas H. *Affluenza.* Berrett-Koehler Publishers, San Francisco, CA. 2001.

DeGrandpre, Richard, Ph.D. *Ritalin Nation.* W.W. Norton and Company, New York. 1999.

DePree, Max. *Leadership Is an Art.* Dell Publishing, New York. 1990.

Drew, Bonnie and Drew, Noel. *Fast Cash for Kids.* Career Press, Franklin Lake, NJ. 1995.

Edwards, Paul, Edwards, Sarah and Roberts, Lisa M. *The Entrepreneurial Parent.* Tarcher/Putnam, New York. 2002.

Fay, Jim. *Tickets to Success*. Love and Logic Press, Inc., Golden, CO. 1994.

Foster, Chad. *Teenagers Preparing for the Real World*. Rising Books, Duluth, GA. 1995.

Garbarino, James, PhD. *Lost Boys*. Free Press, New York. 1999.

Garbarino, James, PhD & Bedard, Carol. *Parents Under Seige*. Free Press, New York. 2001.

Gellatly, Angus and Zarate, Oscar. *Introducing Mind and Brain*. Totem Books, New York. 1999.

Gookin, Dan & Gookin, Sandra Hardin. *Parenting for Dummies*. Hungry Minds, NY. 2002.

Harken, Tom. *The Millionaire's Secret*. Thomas Nelson Publishers, Nashville. 1998.

Harrison, Harry H., Jr. *Father to Son*. Workman, New York, 2000.

Hill, Napoleon. *The Law of Success in Sixteen Lessons*. (Facsimile edition.) Wilshire Book Company, N. Hollywood, CA, 2000.

Iannarelli, Dr. Cindy. *101 Ways to Give Children Business Cents*. Business Cents Resources, Bridgeville, PA. 1998.

Jackson, Tom, M. Ed. *Activities That Teach*. Red Rock Publishing, Cedar City, UT. 1993.

Johnson, Spencer, M.D. *Who Moved My Cheese?* G.P. Putnam's Sons, New York. 1998.

Kiyosaki, Robert T. and Lechter, Sharon L. *Rich Dad, Poor Dad*. Warner Business Books, New York. 1997.

Levine, Mel, M.D. *A Mind at a Time*. Simon & Schuster, New York. 2002.

Lopez, Charlotte and Dworkin, Susan. *Lost in the System*. Simon & Schuster, New York. 1996.

Mackoff, Dr. Barbara. *Growing a Girl*. Dell Publishing, New York. 1996.

McCarty, Oseola. *Simple Wisdom for Rich Living*. Longstreet Press, Atlanta, GA. 1996.

McCullough, Bonnie Runyon and Monson, Susan Walker. *401 Ways to Get Your Kids to Work at Home*. St. Martin's Press, New York. 1981.

Miller, Robert M., D.V.M. *Imprint Training*. Western Horseman Inc., Colorado Springs, CO. 1991.

Modu, Emmanuel. *The Lemonade Stand*. Bob Adams, Inc., Holbrook, MA. 1991.

Murray, Charles. *Human Accomplishment*. Harper Collins, New York. 2003.

Nolte, Dorothy Law and Harris, Rachel. *Children Learn What they Live*. Workman Publishing, New York. 1998.

Pantley, Elizabeth. *Hidden Messages*. Contemporary Books, Chicago, IL. 2001.

Pantley, Elizabeth. *Perfect Parenting*. Contemporary Books, Chicago, IL. 1999.

Ricker, Audrey, Ph.D. and Crowder, Carolyn, Ph.D. *Backtalk*. Fireside, New York. 1998.

Rogers, Fred. *The Mister Rogers Parenting Book*. Running Press, Philadelphia, PA. 2002.

Salamon, Julie. *Rambam's Ladder*. Workman, New York. 2003.

Sanborn, Mark. *The Fred Factor*. Currency-Doubleday, New York. 2004.

Sears, William, M.D. and Sears, Martha, R.N. *The Successful Child*. Little, Brown and Company, Boston, New York, London. 2002.

Schaefer, Dick. *Choices and Consequences*. Hazelden Foundation, Minneapolis, MN. 1998

Sheehy, Harry. *Raising a Team Player*. Storey Books, North Adams, MA. 2002.

Sturtevant, William T. *The Artful Journey*. Bonus Books, Inc., Chicago, IL. 1997.

Templeton, John Marks. *Worldwide Laws of Life, 200 Eternal Spiritual Principles*. Templeton Foundation Press, Philadelphia & London. 1997.

Thomas, David R. *Dave's Way*. Berkley Books, New York. 1991.

Vollbracht, James. *Stopping at Every Lemonade Stand*. Penguin Books, New York. 2001.

Von Oech, Roger. *A Whack on the Side of the Head*. Warner Books, New York. 1993.